The Great Western Railway in Mid Cornwall

Alan Bennett

Published by

Runpast Publishing

10 Kingscote Grove, Cheltenham, Gloucestershire GL51 6JX

Spring-time by the water. '1400' class 0-4-2 tank, No. 1468, leaves Golant for Lostwithiel in the early afternoon of 3rd April 1961. Golant was the only intermediate stop on the branch, opening on 1st July 1896, and closing on 4th January 1965. During World War Two the branch itself closed for three separate periods between January 1940 and October 1944. Temporary closure also took place for a period of seven months in 1917 as a result of World War One. China clay traffic still operates between Lostwithiel and Carne Point maintaining the railway presence at Golant. *P. Gray*

Contents

To my mother,
Doris Bennett

Introduction

Under the G.W.R. Mid Cornwall was served by an extensive rail network. Taking Mid Cornwall to be the area west of Lostwithiel on the main line reaching down to the Redruth/Camborne district, it is a location of contrasting landscapes, history and economic activity.

The main line alone could well warrant a book to itself, but the branches, some still open, many now closed, are also covered for their part in the story overall. Branches to Falmouth, to Newquay and to Fowey, not forgetting, of course, the extensive system serving the clay district gave this part of the county an interesting identity in railway terms. These branches played a vital role in economic growth locally, and, together with the main line, carried considerable traffic of many kinds opening up often otherwise remote rural areas.

The china clay industry, a veritable Cornish giant, dominates to the east, whilst westward there are the extensive remains of the once great copper and tin mining industry. Both these concerns are separated, between Truro and Burngullow, by one of Cornwall's and, indeed, the West Country's finest rural landscapes. Grampound Road station, now closed, once served this vast rural area handling considerable agricultural traffic.

Cornwall is famous for its spectacular coastline and both the north and south coasts offer scenery second to none. They each have their distinctive character. Whilst the north is rugged, grand, and often austere and never to be taken lightly, the south is softer, a more gentle landscape of woodland and pasture, beautiful rivers and estuaries. Newquay on the north coast is now Cornwall's leading holiday resort with a vigorous atmosphere as lively as the winds off the Atlantic itself. Falmouth and Fowey on the south coast offer the tourist a somewhat different experience making much of their maritime heritage. Here, tourism blends successfully with local traditions linking past and present.

Given the contrasts amongst the resorts they frequently compliment one another. This was well understood by the GWR who, from the turn of the century, directed considerable time and money into the creation of what, they considered, was Britain's premier holiday area. The creation of the 'Holiday Line', the 'Ocean Coast' and the ideal of the 'Cornish Riviera' gave the county its distinct identity and appeal. "Come to Cornwall" was an invitation to visit not merely one amongst many tourist areas, but **the** holiday area.

Having assumed effective control of the broad gauge network west of Bristol (from February 1876) the Great Western rapidly became a definitive feature of the life and landscape of the West Country. Be it holiday trains with visitors eager for Cornwall's coast, heavily laden china clay trains for distant markets, or milk, fish and agricultural traffic for London, the Midlands or the North, the Great Western provided the service.

No. 6870 *Bodecote Grange* enters Truro from the west heading the 6.10 pm stopping service from Penzance on 8th July 1961. This excellent view gives a useful indication of Truro's former importance as a railway centre with the locomotive shed in the background and Truro West signalbox to the right. A Hawksworth '9400' class 0-6-0 rests between shunting duties in the foreground. The photograph also illustrates the considerable excavation work carried out at Truro for the main line westward and the construction of the locomotive depot and yard.

P. Gray

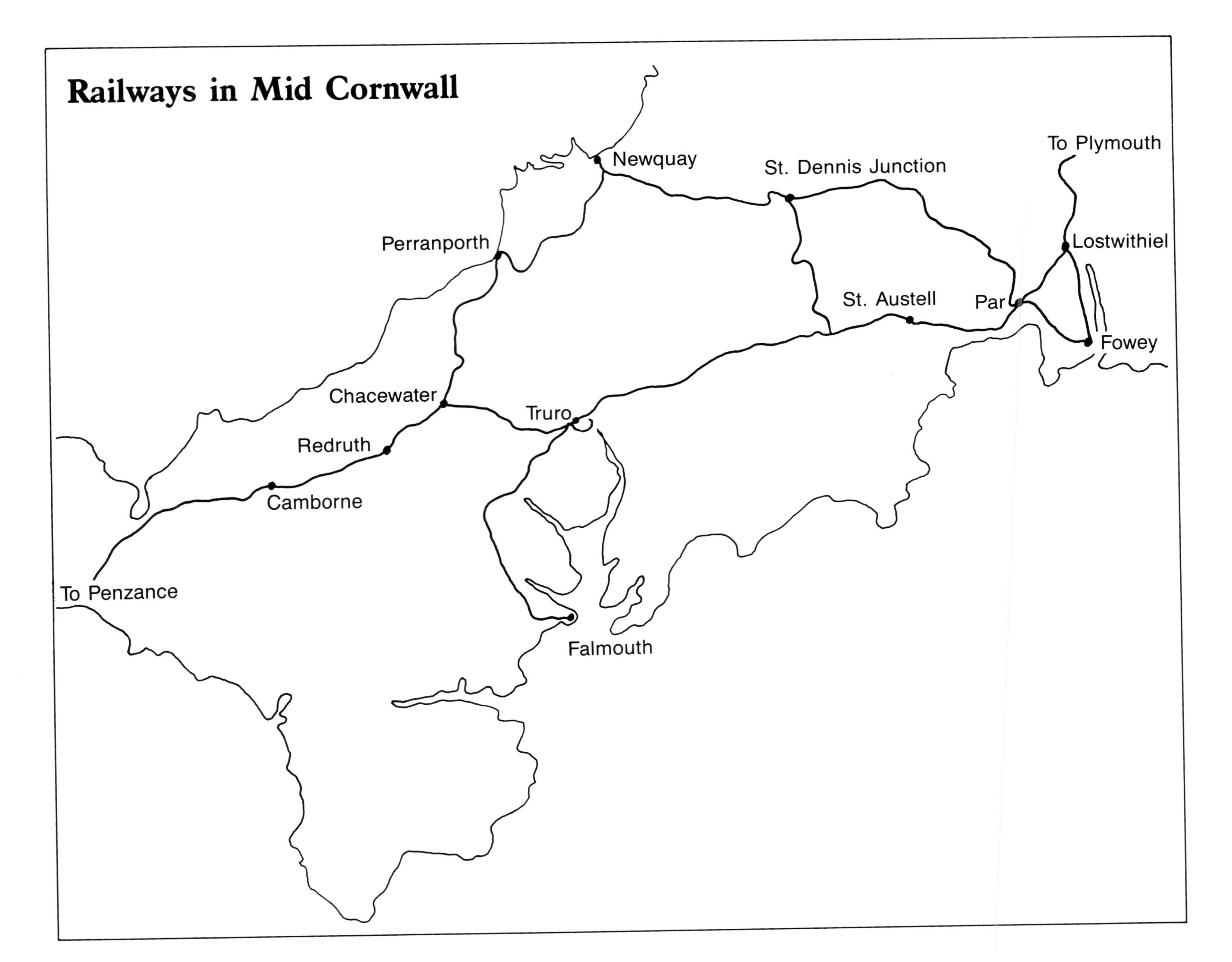
Railways in Mid Cornwall
Newquay
St. Dennis Junction
To Plymouth
Lostwithiel
Perranporth
St. Austell
Par
Fowey
Chacewater
Truro
Redruth
Camborne
To Penzance
Falmouth

Chapter One

The Main Line: Lostwithiel - Truro

Lostwithiel has enjoyed a long and distinguished history reaching back well into the Middle Ages. During the late thirteenth century, under the direction of Edmund, Earl of Cornwall, the town flourished as an administrative and commercial centre, drawing on its mining interests, markets and thriving river port.

The passage of time gradually worked against this earlier prosperity, but by the mid nineteenth century, with railway development proceeding through the county, there was definite optimism for the future. In welcoming the Cornwall Railway's main line from Plymouth to Truro in May 1859, the people of Lostwithiel recognised the opportunity presented them. Together with the obvious advantages that followed for any town finding itself on the main line, the Cornwall Railway also chose to locate its main workshops at Lostwithiel alongside the station. Further development with the opening of the Lostwithiel and Fowey Railway in June 1869 added to the prospects locally, despite the threat to river traffic. This line actually stopped short of Fowey, at Carne Point, where new quays were built for mineral traffic, mainly clay. (See later chapter for details.)

Without doubt the railway opened a new chapter for Lostwithiel and the surrounding area. It also brought detailed changes to the landscape, over-shadowing the town's earlier identity as a busy river port.

The river actually separated railway and town. The station and workshops were to the east and were bounded to the north by the main road, and to the south, by the River Fowey curving round south-eastward. Station accommodation was built by Messrs Olver and Sons of Falmouth who carried out many such contracts for the Cornwall Railway. The main buildings were on the 'up' side and were of wood. In the yard close by, and also on the 'up' side, was the goods shed. It too was of wooden construction, being built to the generous dimensions required of the broad gauge company. Both these structures survived into the 1980s, long after the demise of the Great Western Railway; the station building remaining until 1981, ('up' side) and the goods shed, until the following year. The Cornwall Railway's workshops were also on the 'up' side, set back towards the river-bank. These premises comprised lifting sheds, paint shops, smiths' and carpenters' shops, machine shops, stores and offices. They were, of course, a welcome source of employment and an obvious boost to the local economy, and even after their closure, the GWR remained the principle employer in the 1920s.

Sunshine and showers at Lostwithiel. This fine view westward during the inter-war years offers plenty of detail from this magnificent GWR location. A locomotive is shunting a clay wagon on the 'up' main line whilst the shunter himself, complete with his waterproof and pole, watches from the 'down' side. Lostwithiel was well known for its palm trees and the general abundance of greenery, but note also the excellent gas lamps and the overall standard of maintenance at the station. Even today, in much less attractive surroundings, Lostwithiel still boasts a good floral display on the 'up' platform. The photograph is a period-piece portraying the GWR at its height of achievement. *Redruth Local Studies Library*

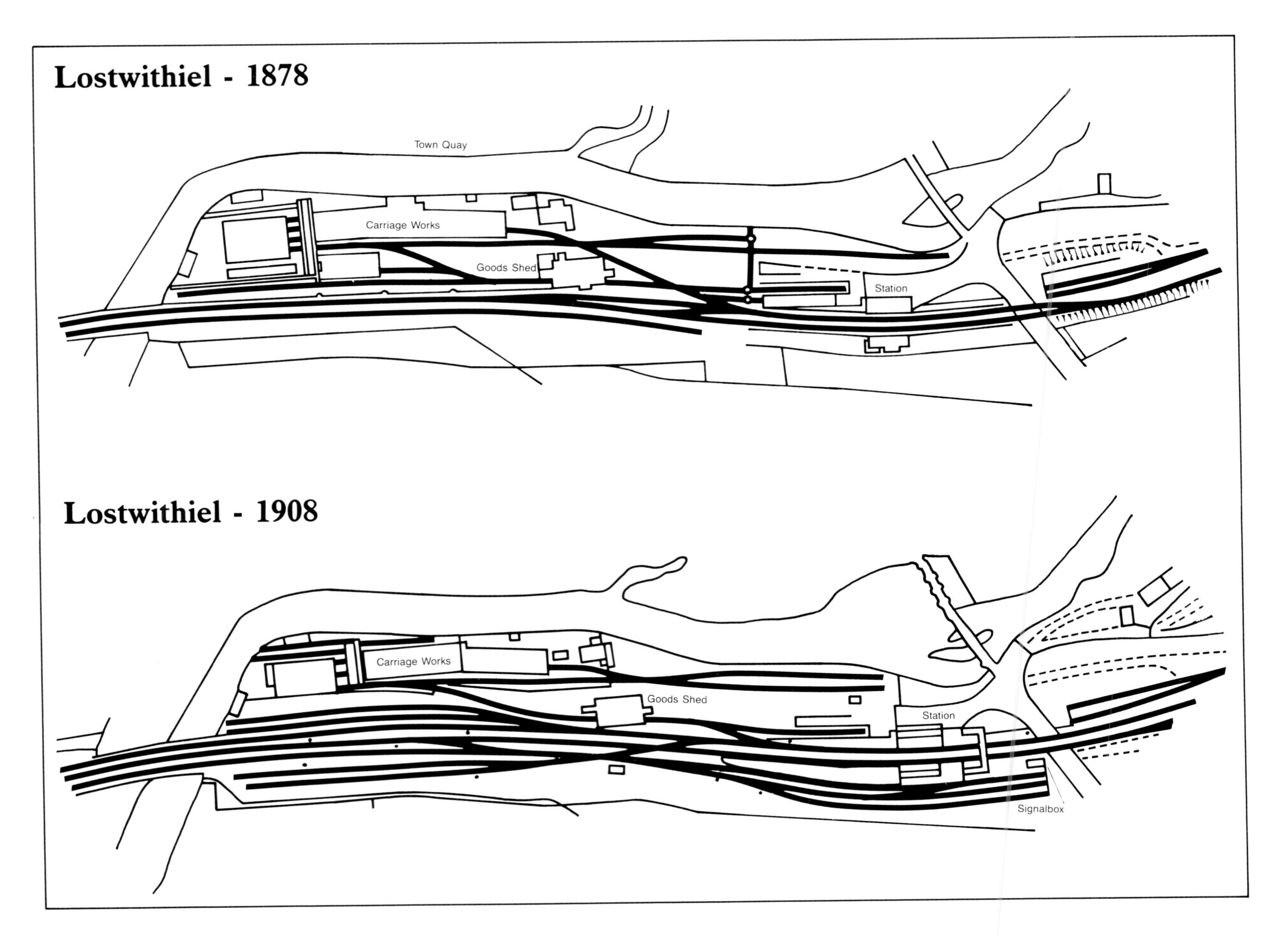
Lostwithiel - 1878
Town Quay
Carriage Works
Goods Shed
Station
Lostwithiel - 1908
Carriage Works
Goods Shed
Station
Signalbox

Lostwithiel was an extensive and busy location by the turn of the century. The 1908 plan shows a number of new sidings, east of the main line, for clay traffic; it also shows the new branch platform for passenger traffic to Fowey, begun in 1895, when the line reopened. To the north, beyond the level crossing, sidings were installed off the 'up' and 'down' lines. Those on the 'up' side were eventually to serve the Nestles Milk Depot opened alongside the 'up' line in 1932. A goods loop was added during World War Two. Sidings on the 'down' side were also later improved with the addition of a goods loop shortly before World War Two. Milk traffic therefore became another valuable source of revenue along with clay movements at Lostwithiel. Increases in freight movement during World War Two, in particular the bulk of the clay traffic, meant that siding space and ease of movement was at a premium. The inevitable growth in traffic through to the post war years was clearly expressed by the fact that, whereas in 1908 there were two sidings alongside the branch platform, there were five by the time nationalisation took place.

Activity at the east end of Lostwithiel's 'up' platform, this time in June 1956. The photograph, taken from the footbridge, captures the lively atmosphere of the railway at work. The engine crew of No. 6821 *Leaton Grange*, take their train away on the climb through the Fowey Valley to Bodmin Road and eastward to Plymouth. *Leaton Grange* has steam to spare and is watched away by interested spectators, whilst two railwaymen in the foreground are in conversation. Road traffic waits at the level crossing. A water crane, lamps, cast iron notice boards, semaphore signals and the signalbox itself maintain the atmosphere of the Great Western. Little, in fact, had changed since nationalisation. *M. Mensing*

Finally, before leaving the survey of Lostwithiel as a railway centre, it is necessary to make reference to two further points. The first is to record that there were two signalboxes controlling movement at the station and yard prior to World War One. That at the north end of the 'down' platform was the most important, also controlling the level crossing alongside. The second box was to the east of the main line opposite the goods shed on the 'down' side, and was closed in the years following World War One.

The second noteworthy point concerns the proposals of 1908 to install water troughs east of the station at Restormel. Water troughs at this location, a relatively level section for mid Cornwall, were considered as a means of improving the performance of express workings such as the 'Cornish Riviera Express' and the numerous fish specials from West Cornwall. Lostwithiel was often the only stop on an otherwise through run for the special fish trains in order to take on water. The water troughs did not materialise but Lostwithiel continued to be a useful watering point for certain eastbound workings until the end of steam working in 1962. All eastbound workings from Lostwithiel, of course, faced a gruelling nine-mile ascent through Bodmin Road to the summit at Doublebois.

Leaving Lostwithiel and running westward, the main line and branch run parallel for a short distance, crossing the River Fowey and then separating. The main line then begins its climb towards Treverrin tunnel almost two miles distant. Whilst the Fowey branch follows a leisurely and extremely beautiful run along the west bank of the magnificent River Fowey, the main line strikes inland somewhat on gradients at 1 in 57, 1 in 62 and 1 in 64 to Treverrin tunnel, where they ease to 1 in 85.

Just over a mile beyond Lostwithiel the line begins to turn south-westward crossing Milltown viaduct. As with most other Cornwall Railway viaducts it was built of wood resting on masonry piers. Milltown was rebuilt of masonry in 1896 and stands 167 yards long and 75 feet high. Double-track working commenced between Lostwithiel and the viaduct on 31st May 1896. A little over a mile beyond comes Treverrin tunnel with the line still climbing.

Before entering the tunnel Treverrin signalbox was passed on the 'up' side. The tunnel itself, 565 yards long, gave its builders their fair share of problems. They found it to be extremely wet, with the extra work required in drainage causing delays in the progress overall on this section of line. Beyond the tunnel the line falls first at 1 in 62 for almost a mile then descends at just over 1 in 100 increasing to 1 in 84 almost to sea level at Par. The section from the west end of Milltown viaduct to Par was doubled in December 1894.

From being no more than a through station on the Cornwall Railway in 1859, Par became an important junction by 1879. In the latter year the GWR opened its double track loop from the Cornwall Minerals Railway (Newquay – Fowey) to the Cornwall Company's (GWR) station on the main line. This enabled passenger services on the standard gauge 'Minerals' system to work from Newquay into Par alongside the broad gauge line from Plymouth westward.

The Newquay services used the island platform alongside the 'up' line from Truro to Plymouth. The broad gauge connection, a facing point at the north end of the station, ran across into the goods shed in the yard west of the main line, enabling an exchange for freight traffic. The main station buildings were on the 'down' side giving easy access from the station approach to the roads from Par Green and Tywardreath in particular. A signalbox was also provided at the south end of the station off the 'up' island platform. No footbridge was provided.

The station was largely rebuilt in 1884 giving much improved accommodation as befitted a busy junction. In 1892, of course, the broad gauge was abolished by the GWR, greatly improving traffic arrangements on and off the branch. Under the rebuilding, revealed in the 1908 plan, Par gained new station accommodation on its 'up' and 'down' platforms. The main buildings, still on the 'down' side, benefitted from a much enlarged station approach allowing road traffic far more room for movement. Both platforms were extended southward immediately next to the signalbox. Goods accommodation was also increased in the yard whilst new sidings were installed on the 'up' side. The latter occupied an extremely marshy area forming the eastern base of a triangle of sorts made up by railway development between the GWR and the CMR in the 1870s.

Looking southward to Par docks and the sea, the railway is lifted over the marshland to cross the Minerals line to Fowey, the main road to St Austell and the river, by means of a low granite viaduct. Looking inland the CMR line runs alongside St Blazey locomotive depot/works and through the yard. This line formed

'1400' class, No. 1419, propels its train into Lostwithiel on the 5.40 pm service from Fowey. The main line can be seen in the background and the River Fowey runs alongside the branch line itself. Passenger services to Fowey began on 16th September 1895, but freight traffic had been operated to Carne Point over the broad gauge from June 1869 to 31st December 1879. The 5½ mile branch saw heavy clay traffic and remains open today for that purpose. The branch was subject to several temporary closures in wartime. In World War One it was closed from 2nd April 1917 to 1st November 1917; during World War Two it was closed for three separate periods between January 1940 and October 1944.
P.Q. Treloar

Above: The railway in the landscape. Peter Gray's excellent panoramic view eastward from Treverrin tunnel. Only the wretched pylons intrude here as a 'County' 4-6-0 climbs westward towards the tunnel mouth. Further down the gradient, towards Lostwithiel, is Milltown viaduct adding to the aesthetic appeal of this pastoral landscape. The photograph also illustrates the former alignment of the single track Cornwall Railway on leaving Treverrin tunnel. Marked by the platelayers' hut, the track bed followed the line of the trees running behind the signalbox to rejoin the present alignment west of the viaduct.

2nd August 1958. *P. Gray*

Right: No. 5915 *Trentham Hall* climbs past Treverrin box, shortly before entering Treverrin tunnel with the 11.05 am stopping train from Plymouth to Penzance on 13th June 1956. The gradient here is 1 in 64.
M. Mensing

Watched by passengers waiting on the 'down' platform, Nos. 7820 *Dinmore Manor* and 6837 *Forthampton Grange* arrive at Par with the SO 11.10 am Penzance – Wolverhampton on 2nd July 1960. The photograph is an excellent study of a Great Western junction station; with the Newquay line curving away to the right alongside the signalbox and water tower. This curve was first opened in January 1879 to link the original Cornwall Railway main line with the Cornwall Minerals Railway. The link itself was standard gauge whilst the main line was, of course, broad gauge until May 1892.
P. Gray

Par station from the west end of the 'down' platform. No. 6849 *Walton Grange* stands at the head of the 7.35 am Newton Abbot – Penzance, whilst No. 5526 waits at the branch platform with a train for Newquay. The large goods shed is seen here behind the branch service. As the station nameboard says, passengers for the nearby Carlyon Bay Hotel were to alight at Par. 12th June 1956.
M. Mensing

the second side of the triangle; the third side was made up by the GWR loop of 1879 linking the two railways.

The main line westward from Par offers great contrasts in scenery. Together with extensive evidence of the china clay industry, there are coastal views across St Austell Bay and an attractive rural setting which characterises the line between Burngullow and Truro.

From Par the line climbs fiercely for six miles to a summit at Burngullow. The gradients are in the 1 in 60s almost all the way to St Austell and required great care and consideration especially on the part of the eastbound heavy clay trains. A cautionary tale from the 1870s makes for a case in point.

On 29th October 1872 a serious collision was narrowly avoided near Par when an eastbound clay train ran out of control west of St Austell. This was a working of some 150 tons headed by the locomotive *Tornado*. The train left Burngullow at 4.20 pm and was due to cross with the 'down' north Mail at St Austell, but, to the great horror of both staff and passengers awaiting their train, the clay working failed to stop. *The West Briton* recounted:

> '. . . the mail was known to have left Par seven minutes previously and it seemed inevitable that the two trains should meet engine to engine with frightful force. But the station officials were as powerless as the passengers to avert the impending disaster, and with one consent they began to run along the line, following the clay train, to witness the catastrophe they feared.'

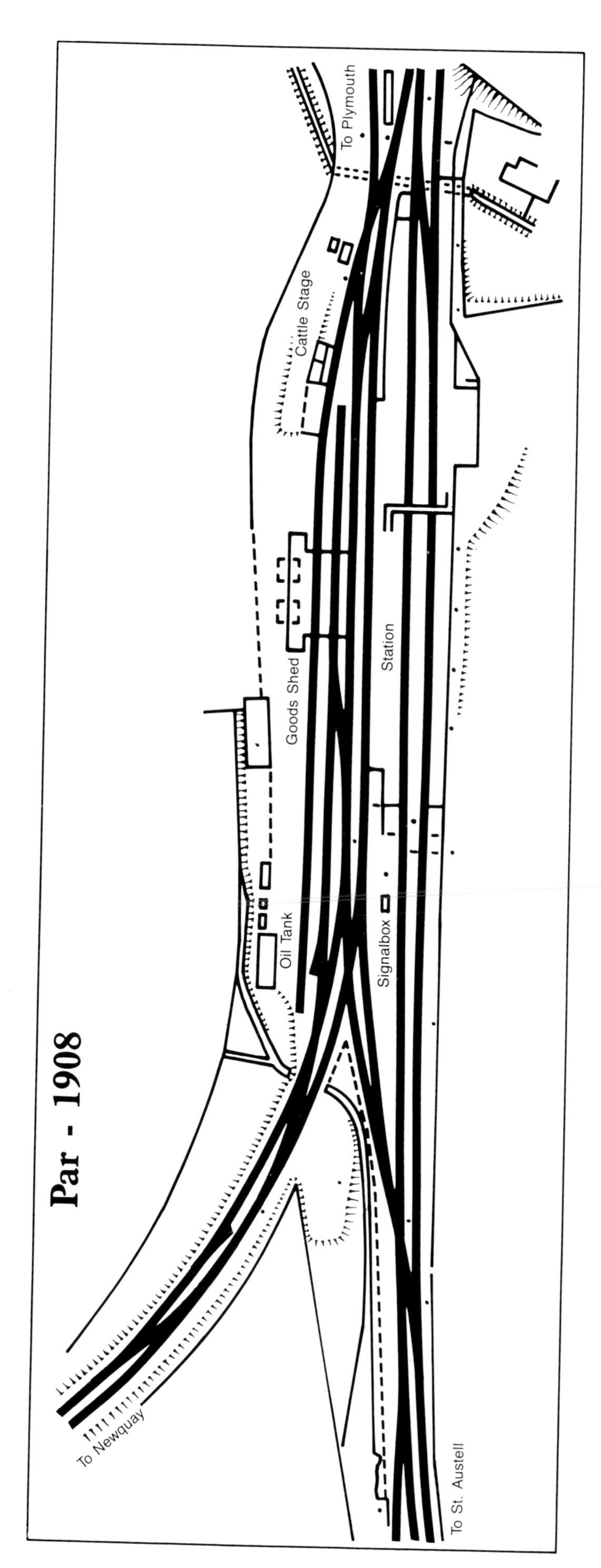

'Par change for Newquay'. Fitted with double chimney, 'County' class 4-6-0 No. 1002 *County of Berks* brings the 'up' 'Cornishman' into Par on 18th May 1959. This train was the 10.10 am Penzance to Wolverhampton and was frequently assigned to a 'County' prior to dieselisation. The branch platform for Newquay, and the curve leading away to St Blazey, can be seen here together with the signalbox, semaphores and a water tower. Note the fierce gradient at 1 in 60 on the westbound route to St Austell. The branch curve was opened on 1st January 1879 in the attempt to improve links between the former Cornwall Minerals Company and the Cornwall Railway's main line. Until May 1892 standard gauge trains to and from Newquay ran into the branch platform at Par, connecting with broad gauge services on the main line. Both main line and branch platforms, seen here, were extended in 1924.

M. Mensing

Climbing well between Par and St Austell, No. 5972 *Olton Hall* has just passed beneath the overbridge east of St Austell golf course. The passengers on this 11.10 am Swansea – Penzance working will have shortly an opportunity to enjoy excellent coastal views across St Austell Bay to the south with Gribben Head lighthouse prominent on the headland. *P. Gray*

Driver Samuel Westlake in charge of the westbound mail sighted the clay train rushing downward towards him on the single track section about a mile east of St Austell. Westlake's response was immediate. He stopped his train, then reversed it back down the gradient, pursued by the clay train. Returning to *The West Briton's* account: 'The passengers were by this time aware, more or less clearly, of the position; some shrieked others fainted, and the boldest was alarmed at the possible issue of the terrible chase . . .' In the event, the trains came to within twenty yards of each other before the mail train began drawing away to safety. Driver Westlake was accordingly the subject of much praise from all concerned, the passengers 'overwhelming him with thanks and pressing gifts on his acceptance'.

The Par – St Austell section was much improved from 15th October 1893 with the provision of double track, thereby removing the possibility of a repeat of the earlier incident. It was also reported that, following the runaway described here, clay trains leaving the Newquay and Cornwall Junction branch at Burngullow were to stop on entry to the level section of main line to pin down brakes. Stop-board notices were also to be given the strictest obedience.

St Austell rapidly became the commercial centre of the china clay industry. The station was on high ground north of the town and handled extensive passenger and goods traffic. St Austell was also the home of a large brewery known throughout the county – a valued source of revenue for the railway. Goods accommodation was originally in the station yard south of the line with entry from the west. This proved inadequate for the demands of trade and in 1931 new and extensive premises were opened, east of the station and to the north of the line. The main buildings in the station were on the 'down', south side. Immediately behind the 'up' platform there was also a loading platform served by two sidings with a third beyond running the length of the station. Access was from the east, where, at the end of the platform, were cattle pens. St Austell signalbox was to the extreme west of the station area on the north side of the line.

Shortly after leaving St Austell the junction for the GWR Lansalson branch led away northward on a facing connection. This branch opened to china clay traffic in May 1920 serving several clay producers along the course of the Trenance Valley. St Austell viaduct follows. Built on a curve at 240 yards long and 115 feet high, it was rebuilt in masonry in 1898. Trenance Dries were also north of the line immediately beyond the viaduct. They were coal fired and were served by sidings alongside. Climbing on a gradient largely at 1 in 84 the line next reaches Gover viaduct just over a mile west of St Austell. Like St Austell viaduct this

St Austell has always been considered the commercial centre of the china clay industry, and, therefore, one of mid Cornwall's most important towns. Here, No. 5987 *Brocket Hall* leaves the station with a summer season working for Penzance in the late 1950s. This view from the west shows a busy if somewhat overcrowded site which led the GWR to open, during 1931, a new goods yard east of the station in far more spacious surroundings.
P.Q. Treloar

With St Austell in the background, No. 6823 *Oakley Grange* crosses St Austell viaduct itself with a westbound train of empty coaching stock on 6th August 1959. The viaduct was rebuilt in 1898, and at the far end, curving away to the left, is the Lansalson clay branch opened by the GWR in May 1920.
P. Gray

7921

6809

was originally a timber structure resting on stone piers. At 230 yards long and 95 feet high, Gover was also replaced in 1898.

A short level section ending at Burngullow, just over two miles west of St Austell, marks the western limit of the china clay district. China clay dries were built at Burngullow and, today, they cover an extensive area immediately to the north of the line. The Newquay and Cornwall Junction Railway, opened in July 1869, leads away northward into the clay producing district opposite the site of Burngullow signalbox and the now closed Burngullow station. The clay branch is described in some detail elsewhere and it is sufficient here to note that it linked the main line with St Dennis Junction, between Newquay and Par. In August 1901 Burngullow station was resited; the 'down' platform being opposite the branch and the 'up' platform, considerably shorter, being alongside the junction. A small one-road locomotive shed also stood north of the line. The station eventually closed to all traffic in September 1931. The original structure, opened by the Cornwall Railway in 1863, was a short distance to the east. Double track was provided between St Austell and Burngullow from 26th March 1899.

'Castle' class No. 5069 *Isambard Kingdom Brunel* heads westward with the heavily loaded 8.20 am Paddington – Perranporth on 8th July 1961. The train has just crossed Coombe St Stephens viaduct, rebuilt in 1886, and is seen leaving the china clay district with the distinctive waste tips in the background.
P. Gray

Opposite top: Modified 'Hall' No. 7921 *Edstone Hall* climbs away from the St Austell district with the 11.10 am Swansea – Penzance on 6th August, 1959. The locomotive and leading coaches have just crossed Gover viaduct, rebuilt 1898, whilst beyond, partially obscured by the exhaust, can be seen Trenance china clay dries, and in the far distance, St Austell viaduct.
P. Gray

Opposite bottom: An 'up' express enters St Austell behind No. 6809 *Burghclere Grange*. Both the east and west approaches to the station were noted for the abundant trees and rhodedendrons at the lineside. The 'Granges' and 'Halls' were ideal motive power for all types of work on the Cornish main line; their mixed traffic status being suitable for passenger, parcels or perishable workings. With a 60 mph speed limit imposed on the main line these locomotives found no difficulties with the steep gradients, curvature and the numerous stops associated with the line through the county. 'Granges' were permitted maximum loads of 385 tons on the Cornish main line; 'Halls' were allowed 380 tons, and 'Castles', 420 tons.
P.Q. Treloar

Grampound Road, looking eastward during the 1920s. The station was sited largely in a cutting with the goods shed and main buildings situated at the east end of the platform. An 'up' refuge siding was provided at the west end of the station in 1898; the 'down' refuge being to the east of the site opposite the small goods yard. Before the introduction of rail services to Newquay a horse bus provided a service between the resort and the station at Grampound, travelling via St Columb. Grampound Road also served a widespread and rich agricultural district, handling a great deal of traffic in livestock and produce. *Redruth Local Studies Library*

The onset of diesel working. Swindon-built Bo-Bo diesel hydraulic D802 *Formidable* of the 'Warship' class has just passed Grampound Road station with the 9.15 am Penzance – Plymouth on Whit Monday 1959. The goods yard, following the curve, is seen to the right of the train. These locomotives quickly assumed control of the major trains through the county – 'The Cornish Riviera', 'The Cornishman', and 'The Royal Duchy'. *M. Mensing*

Right: Probus and Ladock Halt in the 1920s. This view eastward shows the simple provision offered here with wooden platforms, corrugated iron shelters and oil lamps. The halt served a widespread rural area, opening in February 1908 and closing in December 1957. The soldier and the young ladies on the 'down' platform add interest; likewise, the lady passenger sitting in the sunshine awaiting the train.

Redruth Local Studies Library

Below: A meeting at milepost 298¾, east of Buckshead tunnel. No. 6808 *Beenham Grange*, on the westbound Ealing Broadway–Penzance passes No. 1024 *County of Pembroke* on the 2.00 pm Penzance–Crewe 'Perishable'. The curvature on the main line is evident here as the line turns eastward towards Polperro tunnel. 2nd August 1958. *P. Gray*

Leaving the china clay district, the line falls for more than two miles to Coombe St Stephen viaduct, 246 yards long and 70 feet high. It was rebuilt in 1886. Half a mile beyond, the Fal viaduct is reached. At 190 yards in length and 90 feet high this structure was rebuilt in 1884. The River Fal passing beneath is of almost insignificant proportion in comparison to its size further down river where it opens out in a magnificent spectacle. Climbing again for a further two miles the line enters Grampound Road.

Grampound Road served a widespread and productive agricultural community bringing valuable returns in livestock, general agricultural traffic, and, in earlier years, small amounts of china clay. Prior to the opening of the CMR passenger services in 1876 Grampound served as the railhead for passengers to Newquay. Coach services linked the station with the north coast resort, travelling via St Columb. The once busy goods yard was to the east of the station, north of the line with sidings also being provided opposite, on the 'down' side. Grampound Road was one

Another view between Buckshead and Polperro tunnels. Here Nos. 6913 *Levens Hall*, and 7816 *Frilsham Manor*, head westward to Buckshead with the 'down' 'Cornish Riviera Express' on 2nd August 1958. This photograph shows also the original alignment of the Cornwall Railway on the grassed section to the right of the train. *P. Gray*

of many more minor stations to close in October 1964 under the impact of the Beeching Axe. Double track working was introduced eastward to Burngullow on 22nd May 1898.

A further two-mile descent, mostly at 1 in 67, carries the line past the sites of Probus viaduct and Probus and Ladock Platform. The latter opened in February 1908, serving a widespread but sparsely populated agricultural area. It closed in December 1957. Probus viaduct, 145 yards long and 43 feet high, was replaced by an embankment in 1871. The entire section from Probus eastward to Burngullow was singled during 1986, making this the longest of the three sections of single track now in operation west of the Tamar. Originally, this section was doubled (Probus to Grampound Road) on 3rd April 1898. Two further viaducts, Tregarne and Tregeagle, 202 yards long and 83 feet high and 105 yards long and 69 feet high respectively, both rebuilt in 1902, mark the climb to Polperro Tunnel. At 581 yards this was the second longest tunnel in the county, exceeded only by St Pinnock on the CMR route between Par and Fowey. A descent through the tunnel and the abounding rural landscape on both sides of the line, followed by a climb of ¾ of a mile, brings the entrance to Buckshead Tunnel, 320 yards length. Buckshead marks the site of the ceremonial cutting of the first sod on the Cornwall Railway in August 1847. The section between the tunnels was opened to double-track working on 15th October 1899. From Buckshead Tunnel there follows a continuous descent, largely at 1 in 78 for a mile to Truro viaduct. At 92 feet high and 443 yards long the latter was clearly Cornwall's lengthiest viaduct; it was also rebuilt in brick, resting on granite piers, a most unusual practice in Cornwall. The original masonry piers of the timber viaduct still stand alongside the present structure on the 'down', south side. With Truro and its river reaching away to the south of the line, Carvedras viaduct followed, leading into Truro station itself. Carvedras, 323 yards long and 86 feet high, was replaced in 1902; Truro viaduct was rebuilt in 1904.

Chapter Two

Truro - Cornwall's Railway Centre

Truro is the commercial and cultural capital of Cornwall and the county's only cathedral town. Throughout the last century, as today, it promoted a purposeful, prosperous image as a mercantile and administrative centre drawing on its links with the mining industry and its role as a market town and river port. By the mid-nineteenth century the town was also heavily committed to railway development within the county; its ideal position, geographically, being of great significance for transport and trade.

A major initiative for Truro and other associated towns along the county's south coast came on 3rd August 1846. On that day both the Cornwall and West Cornwall Railways, serving Truro from the east and west, were incorporated under Acts of Parliament. Truro was the obvious administrative centre for both companies; the first official meeting of the Cornwall Railway being held in the town on 16th December 1846.

A view of the rebuilt Truro station at the turn of the century. Truro gained a prestigious new station in 1898, which, unlike most Cornish stations was built of brick. This view shows the new station looking eastward with 'Bulldog' 4-4-0 No. 3457 *Tasmania* at platform three. This platform handled the Falmouth services prior to the opening of the branch to Perranporth, 1903 and Newquay 1905. The name board reads, 'Truro change for Falmouth', indicating that the latter branch had not yet opened.
Royal Institution of Cornwall

The Cornwall company was the larger of the two projects, linking across the Tamar to Plymouth and thence to the railway network beyond. Under original proposals the line was to run westward from the South Devon Railway's terminus at Millbay in Plymouth to the terminus at Falmouth. Strict economies, however, dictated by local problems and a decisive financial crisis resulted in the broad gauge single line opening initially to Truro on 4th May 1859.

In the event, the smaller West Cornwall Company was first to open, this being on 25th August 1852. The West Cornwall route to Penzance, 25 miles 11 chains, was also opened as a single line but, significantly, it was built to the standard gauge, 4 feet 8½ inches. Initial services were operated from a temporary terminus known as Truro Road at Highertown, west of the present tunnel. The decision to build to the standard gauge was itself the result of economies, compromises and uncertainties over the future. A letter to the local press in August 1856 signed by 'A Shareholder', for example, advised against the West Cornwall forming too close a relationship with broad gauge interests. The advice was to wait for the London and South Western Railway and its expansion westward. Prior to its Act of Incorporation, the Cornwall company faced direct competition from the rival Cornwall and Devon Central Railway proposed as 'the right railway for the County on both commercial and engineering terms'. The Cornwall Central scheme was finally rejected in favour of the broad gauge coastal route, but not without considerable effort. Even towards the end of the century there were still projects under review supporting the advance of the London and South Western into West Cornwall.

The opening of the West Cornwall line was greeted enthusiastically with the main celebrations being focussed on Penzance. Truro, with its West Cornwall neighbours, was now host to the railway, albeit, looking westward and as yet isolated from the national network.

Initial services on the West Cornwall line, comprising three trains in each direction, weekdays only, were as follows:

Truro	dep	7.38 am	2.00 pm	7.00 pm
Penzance	arr	9.20 am	3.45 pm	8.45 pm
Penzance	dep	8.30 am	12.00	5.00 pm
Truro	arr	10.15 am	1.45 pm	6.45 pm

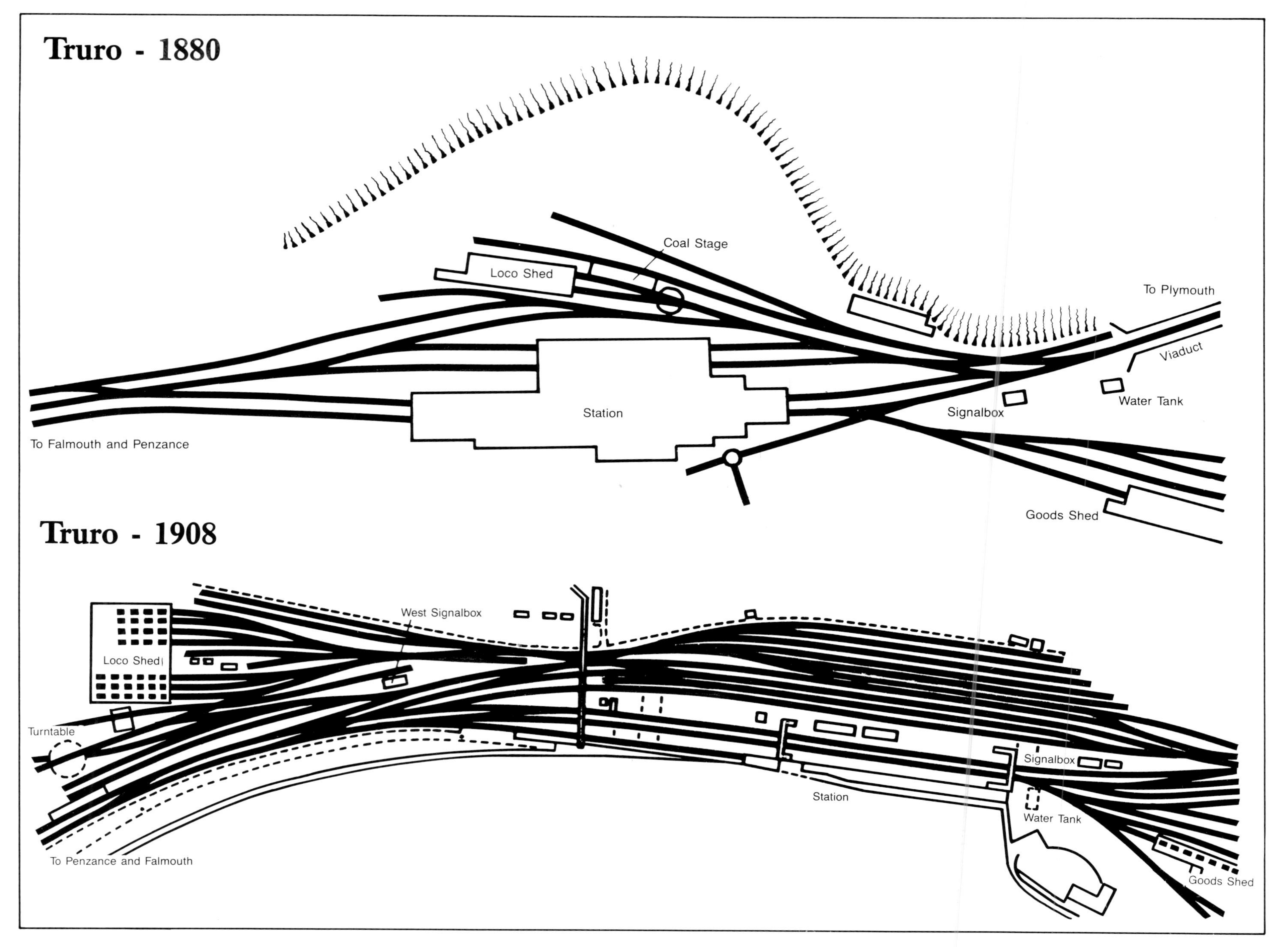
Truro - 1880
Coal Stage
Loco Shed
To Plymouth
Viaduct
Water Tank
Signalbox
Station
To Falmouth and Penzance
Goods Shed
Truro - 1908
West Signalbox
Loco Shed
Turntable
Signalbox
Station
Water Tank
To Penzance and Falmouth
Goods Shed

Trains stopped at all stations and provided first, second and third class accommodation. During the interim, between the opening of the West Cornwall and completion of the Cornwall Railway, the 'Magnet' coach service was one of several offering a road link between Truro and Plymouth. With the opening of the railway through the county, coach fares were reduced considerably in recognition of the competition and threat posed by the new train services.

The West Cornwall Railway terminus at Truro Road closed on 16th April 1855 following the construction of the 2½ mile extension to Newham on the banks of the Truro River. This additional section formed a U shape descent curving around the high ground to the west/south-west of the town. The line followed a southerly course from Penwithers passing over the Truro-Plymouth turnpike, now the A39. Following a creek off the Truro River the line then turned eastward before finally running north along the river bank to the Newham terminus. Powers to build the extension to Newham were obtained in 1853 but not before the West Cornwall Company had come into conflict with Truro Town Council over questions of access and ownership of land at the riverside location. Newham terminus included a wooden passenger station with an overall roof enclosing two sets of tracks. Passenger services at Newham were shortlived, however, as the majority of trains were transferred to the new Cornwall Railway station when opened from 11th May 1859. Closure to passenger services at Newham followed on 16th September 1863.

Completion of the Cornwall Railway to Truro promised prosperity and a new era of progress for the town. Two days before the opening of the single line westward from Plymouth, the Mayor and various local dignitaries travelled from Truro to the official opening of the Royal Albert Bridge across the Tamar. Unfortunately, many of those invited from Cornwall were not able to witness the occasion as the locomotive hauling their train broke a connecting rod at Liskeard making them late for the ceremony. The crossing of the Tamar celebrated on 2nd May 1859 and the official opening of the line itself on 3rd May marked a watershed in the county's development. During the course of much inevitable speech making at the ceremony on 3rd May it was claimed that the line would be 'of incalculable importance, not only to the county, but to the nation at large for both the purposes of war and peace'. (National defences, particularly those along the south coast were of vital importance to the War Office at this time, given fears of French aggression. A continuous rail link running the length of the south coast boosted Britain's defensive capabilities giving the means for rapid and easy movement of men and materials; War Office interests would have, nevertheless, preferred uniformity; in this case, the adoption of standard gauge.) Returning to the detail of the ceremony, the Mayor, Dr Barham, and Corporation stood on one side of the platform whilst the Directors of the Cornwall and Associated Companies (Great Western, Bristol and Exeter and South Devon) assembled on the other, welcoming the official train. The latter, a double-headed working of fourteen coaches, departed Plymouth at 10.20 am carrying approximately 800 passengers and invited guests. Truro, like all other towns along the line, set its clocks to 'London Time'. An announcement by the Cornwall Railway was clear and to the point: 'Greenwich time is kept at all stations. It is 20 minutes earlier than Truro time'. With a break of gauge at Truro it was now possible to enjoy rail travel from Paddington to Penzance. Normal services to the public began on 4th May 1859.

The Cornwall Railway's station was on high ground some distance west of the main area of the town. Despite lacking a central position within the town, the new station obviously pleased the community. The main building and forecourse opened onto Richmond Hill and the road leading westward to Redruth. Described as 'a handsome stone structure, 130 feet long with large projecting roof', the station building clearly made an impact. The booking office, with separate entrances for first, second and third class passengers, occupied the central section, whilst to each side were the first, second and third class waiting rooms, and the parcels rooms, offices and conveniences. Immediately inside the station was the departure platform 161 feet long and 14 feet wide. Three sets of broad gauge rails separated this from the arrival platform 141 feet long and 20 feet wide. The outer platform face here served the standard gauge West Cornwall services. This entire arrangement was given the protection of an overall roof with two clear spans of forty-seven and forty-one feet. Messrs Olver and Son of Falmouth were the contractors and were warmly congratulated by the local press for their 'swift and tasteful efforts on behalf of the town'.

To the north of the station was the locomotive shed almost 100 feet in length and 38 feet wide. It was constructed of timber with a slate roof, and accommodated two sets of tracks. A blacksmith and general workshop was also provided together with coaling facilities and a water tank. This land north of the station originally fell away steeply forming the side of a valley so the new site therefore required considerable infilling and levelling to provide the solid ground for the outer station area and locomotive shed. To the west of the station, it was also necessary to drive Highertown tunnel at 70 yards length through the hill separating the Cornwall and West Cornwall Railways, and to give the necessary access for the Falmouth line. Passenger trains from West Cornwall began using the new Truro station on 11th May 1859.

The goods shed was at the eastern end of the station to the south of the line. It was a masonry structure with good access from the main road nearby. One line entered the goods shed itself with three others serving the yard alongside. The signalbox was positioned between the yard and the main line. Before leaving the layout at the goods yard, mention must also be made of an additional siding running westward off the main line which almost approached the station frontage itself. It was provided with a wagon turntable which enabled a further siding to be placed in at right angles.

With the arrival of the Cornwall Railway, the neighbouring West Cornwall company was obliged by law to provide access for broad gauge trains over its lines to Penzance. This was made clear in the Act of 1850 allowing the West Cornwall to build to the standard gauge with the proviso that it would implement mixed gauge working as and when required. The Cornwall Railway gave official notice of the requirement to do this in 1864 to put an end to the problems and obstructions of the break of gauge at Truro. Break of gauge was a considerable inconvenience to passenger traffic but it was a major problem for freight movement, where time-consuming and costly loading and unloading was required in the transfer of goods from one gauge to the other.

The problem was resolved in two stages: firstly, on 6th November 1866, when the first broad gauge goods train ran through to Penzance – a consignment of wheat from Falmouth – and, secondly, on 1st March 1867 when through passenger workings began between Paddington and Penzance. Prior to the introduction of the mixed gauge, and with the opening of the Falmouth branch in August 1863, two separate gauges ran through Highertown tunnel. Such arrangements contributed much to interest in Truro as a lively and strategic railway centre, as, indeed, did the provision of a mixed gauge working between Truro and Penzance operating from November 1871 to May 1892 when the broad gauge was finally abolished. A crucially important development for railway interests in Cornwall had also taken place in 1876 when the GWR assumed a controlling hand generally on lines from Paddington to the West of England. Its influence overall was decisive.

'4575' class 2-6-2T No. 5552 shunting at Newham Wharf on 20th July 1960. The river, the cathedral and the city can all be seen here; note also the crane for transfer of goods from river to railway, on the wharf itself. This view looks northwards into the city, and towards the terminus at Newham.
R.C. Riley

The 'other' Truro station. Newham terminus on the banks of the Truro River is seen here in Great Western days. Newham was the terminus for the West Cornwall Railway from 16th April 1855 to 11th May 1859. Thereafter it became almost entirely a goods depot. It was a wooden structure with an overall roof which eventually outlived the GWR itself.
Royal Institution of Cornwall

A view eastward from Truro station showing work in progress to replace the original Carvedras viaduct with the new masonry structure. The new viaduct was opened to traffic on 17th August 1902 with double track working commencing in April 1904. *Cornwall County Museum*

No. 6938 *Cordean Hall* crosses Carvedras viaduct to enter Truro station with a 'down' train. this masonry structure replaced the original timber viaduct in August 1902. Heavy engineering was required for the railway to enter Truro. Truro viaduct itself was the longest in Cornwall at 443 yards, and opened in February 1904. To the west a deep cutting and a tunnel at Highertown were required. *P.Q. Treloar*

An unusual view from the east end of Truro station showing the goods shed, and the main line running across Carvedras viaduct. The city and its cathedral (completed in 1907) are well illustrated here and good indication is given of the views enjoyed from trains on the viaduct. Truro viaduct itself is in the far distance with the cattle sidings and signalbox seen on the section separating these two magnificent structures. A new Birmingham RC and W Co. DMU set stands in the sidings. These often worked local services between Plymouth and Penzance and were quite popular with passengers from their introduction in 1960. 8th April 1960. *R.C. Riley*

'Grange' 4-6-0 No. 6836 *Estevarney Grange* passes Truro East Box as it enters the station from the east on 7th July 1955. This signalbox was the only one to survive into the present day; Truro West Box, situated in the yard between the station and the locomotive depot, closed in 1971. *R.C. Riley*

By the turn of the century detailed changes had been made to the station and locomotive departments. During the summer of 1887 *The Cornish Telegraph* described Truro station in less than flattering terms. 'Damp, dismal, dirty, draughty is the general verdict of the travelling public'. It was also claimed that 'only the older company servants could remember when it last received a coat of paint'. Within the next decade reconstruction was underway. In July 1897 the *Royal Cornwall Gazette* commented on the rebuilding programme:

> 'The Railway Station is still undergoing the transforming process. The cloakroom, refreshment room and other offices west of the booking department have been demolished and new and more permanent, as well as more slightly errections will soon rise on that site. The excavation which is of a colossal character at Dobb's Field where the new engine department is to be is progressing toward completion'.

Truro took possession of an excellent new station and locomotive depot to meet the requirements of the twentieth century. The new locomotive shed was immediately east of Highertown tunnel to the north of the line. A great deal of cutting into the hillside and levelling was necessary to complete this project. The original locomotive shed opposite the station was closed in May 1900; the new premises opening at the same time. Built as a three road structure with turntable, coaling stage and workshops it was later enlarged to meet increased demands upon it.

The station was a most impressive structure. All the main buildings were on the 'down' side facing the road. There were four platform faces, number one being a bay later used by Falmouth trains. Platform Two served the 'down' main line, whilst number three, for the Falmouth line, was soon host to the branch services on the newly opened line to Perranporth, in 1903, and, eventually, Newquay in 1905. Platform Four was then used for 'up' main line workings. Two covered footbridges were provided and there were also water columns at the east end of platforms three and four and to the west end of platforms two and three. The platforms at the west end of the station were lengthened soon after the new buildings opened, before, in fact, services began on the Newquay branch. Two signalboxes, Truro East and Truro West, controlled movements overall. The layout in the goods yard east of the station was revised with the removal of the more awkward sidings and the provision of extra lines running north and south of the goods shed. With the removal of the old engine shed there was room for increased siding accommodation north of the station including goods loops. The ticket platform at Truro, a source of considerable delay and annoyance, was also finally removed in 1897.

East of the station, between the two viaducts, a siding was also provided to handle livestock traffic from the cattle market close by. This accommodation consisted of a loop with short sections at each end to store wagons and allow for free movement through the loop. This new arrangement, on the 'down' side, came into use in September 1898, marking a valuable improvement for the livestock trade. Before the new siding was available traffic was heavy. In 1895, for example, over 1,100 wagons of livestock left Truro. A signalbox was opened at the cattle siding in 1904.

As a community generally, Truro also benefitted from several important developments which had taken place by the end of the century. In 1877, for example, the town was given city status and in 1880 work began on the construction of a cathedral. Later in the same decade, the County Councils Act of 1888 resulted in the formation of the Cornwall County Council. Its headquarters were located at Truro. The community was obviously much enhanced by this new and close identification with county administration in both civil and ecclesiastical affairs. Truro's central location and accessibility, as provided by the railway, were crucial factors here in its favour.

With the opening of the Chacewater – Newquay line on 2nd January 1905, Truro's position as an important local railway centre was enhanced. No great changes were made during the inter-war years except, of course, for the continuing improvement in train services, nor did any real change follow from nationalisation. With busy main line services to Paddington, Bristol, the Midlands,

The platforms have been lengthened in this second old view and the paint work generally has been improved, giving the station a much brighter aspect. Note the large new yard gained in the rebuilding programme and the gas tank in what became the Falmouth bay platform. The main road, beyond the station wall, leads down into the city. *Royal Institution of Cornwall*

One of Truro's large allocation of '4500'/'4575' class 2-6-2 pannier tanks leaving with a three-coach train for Newquay in the summer of 1957. The locomotive, No. 4597, is about to enter the deep cutting leading to Highertown tunnel. Beyond the train is the locomotive shed opened in 1900.

Evidence of the heavy engineering needed at the west end of the station. No. 6931 *Aldborough Hall* climbs out of Truro with the west-bound 'Cornish Riviera Express' shortly before that train was taken over by the new diesel hydraulic locomotives of the North British Company. The locomotive on the 'down' 'Limited' returned later in the evening with the Penzance – Paddington Postal, (TPO).

Both, P.Q. Treloar

Half a century later, Churchward mogul No. 6300 stands at platform two with the Falmouth portion of the 9.30 am Paddington – Penzance service. The covered accommodation for the platforms has obviously been extended by comparison with the previous views. The locomotive, seen here, frequently worked local freights and stopping services to Penzance. 18th September 1957. *P.Q. Treloar*

South Wales and the North Country and, of course, reciprocal workings to Penzance, local stopping trains to Plymouth and Penzance and services on the Falmouth and Newquay branches, Truro saw heavy passenger traffic. The goods yards were also kept busy with through freights on the main line, traffic to and from Falmouth, and the local pick-up turns to Camborne and the large yard at Drump Lane, Redruth. Together with these were also the workings to Newham Wharf and the pick-up service on the Newquay Branch. Over one hundred trains, main line and branch workings, used Truro station on summer Saturdays in the late 1950s, excluding empty stock and parcels/perishables.

Truro saw considerable change during the course of the 1960s largely indicative of decline. The locomotive shed closed to steam in September 1962. Many of the depot's locomotives prior to this had been tank engines, mainly the '4500' and '4575' class 2-6-2Ts working the branch passenger and freight turns. '9400' class 0-6-0Ts were also in evidence, again, mainly for shunting but also freight turns and the occasional passenger train on the Falmouth branch. Churchward '4300' class 2-6-0s, the best known in the later years being Nos. 5376 and 6300, were also a feature at Truro, working freight trains and local stopping services to Penzance. 'Halls', 'Granges' and 'Manors' were also present on Truro's books, but pride of place towards the last days of steam went to No. 1023 *County of Oxford*. Not the only 'County' to find a home at Truro, No. 1007 *Count of Brecknock* also appeared regularly; but *County of Oxford* was always immaculately maintained and frequently worked the humble 4.15 pm stopping train from Truro to Penzance in order to return with the 8.45 pm sleeper service to Paddington, considered a prestigious working. The locomotive shed closed entirely in 1965.

Two years earlier, on 4th February 1963, closure came to the Chacewater – Newquay branch, an obvious victim of the Beeching Axe. Truro West signalbox was closed in 1965, with rationalisation also taking place in yard facilities. Early in the following decade, further economies were made with the closure of the goods shed and the relegation of the through line on Platform Four to a siding; buffer stops being installed at the eastern end of the platform. The Newham branch had also by this time passed into history, but the Falmouth branch survives, having been subject to strict economies. Truro is now the westernmost limit for freight working in Cornwall other than for engineers' trains or fuel tankers for Penzance, and the station also acts as an administrative centre for the county's railways. The station still retains a certain sense of importance and whilst it is clearly no longer as busy as in the past it is well maintained, displaying its Great Western Railway ancestory with pride. Platform Three has handled all 'up' main line services for well over a decade; Platform Two dealing with all 'down' main line workings. Branch services to Falmouth still operate from the bay platform offering a certain sense of continuity with the past. The intense pattern of local services once concentrated upon Truro has now virtually disappeared but the station enjoys an excellent standard of Inter-City workings giving direct and swift access to widespread destinations including London, the Midlands, the

Contrasts in motive power at Truro in April 1960. No. 4083 *Abbotsbury Castle* waits in the yard for the road westward whilst '5700' class No. 4622 leaves for Falmouth. A diesel shunter reflects the decline of steam, a great deal of the shunting being previously carried out by the '9400' class 0-6-0 PTs. Truro West Box is also very prominent here. *R.C. Riley*

No. 6800 *Arlington Grange* is seen here in Truro's large goods yard alongside the station on 21st June 1962. Steam power had then only a matter of months left in Cornwall, the locomotive depots closing to steam in September of that year. The locomotive carries a headcode indicating perishable traffic, which would be bound for markets beyond the West Country. *R.C. Riley*

Truro locomotive depot (83F) west of the station on 8th April 1960. The depot had a fair number of '4500' and '4575' 2-6-2Ts for branch and local freight workings with several of them being seen here. The depot opened in 1900 and was closed in 1965. *R.C. Riley*

North and also Scotland. The Western Region's recent and welcome introduction of a Pullman service on the early morning IC 125 Penzance – Paddington and the returning early evening departure from the Capital reflects something of the GWR's particular commitment to high standards of service to and from the county. Truro itself has enjoyed long and close connections with railway interests in Cornwall, and like the city it serves, the station maintains a purposeful and lively atmosphere mindful of its past but looking also to the future.

Steam and diesel workings at Truro in 1959. '4575' class No. 5536 arrives at Truro with the 10.25 am from Falmouth. Two class '22' 1,000 H.P. diesel hydraulics, Nos. D6301 and D6302, are at platform two working the 7.45 am Newton Abbot – Penzance service having taken over from the usual 'Hall' 4-6-0 that had normally been assigned to this train. A 'County' 4-6-0 can be seen in the goods yard waiting to take a fitted freight westward on the main line, whilst a diesel shunter also reflects the changing scene at that time. 21st September 1959. *P.Q. Treloar*

Chapter Three

The Main Line: West of Truro

Running westward from Truro the main line over the route of the old West Cornwall Company is characterised by a series of curves and heavy gradients. The landscape itself differs considerably from that east of Truro. Whereas the latter has a somewhat lush, gentle, appearance, much of the land on the West Cornwall route is of poorer quality following high ground marked on both sides of the line by the extensive remains of copper and tin mining setts. This is particularly the case between Chacewater and Camborne.

The immediate exit from Truro, climbing through Higher-town tunnel to Penwithers Junction has been described in the chapter on the Falmouth branch, and from there the line curves away westward in a wide cutting towards Redruth and Penzance. Immediately beyond Penwithers the line begins to climb for upwards of three miles at 1 in 80. Some ¾ mile beyond the junction is Penwithers viaduct, 124 yards long and 54 feet high. This was originally a timber construction with the later modification of stone piers which did service until 1887 when the structure was rebuilt entirely in masonry. The north, or 'up' side of the line, also shows clear evidence of realignment since the early days of the WCR. With only the shortest of breaks, the gradient sharpens to 1 in 70 towards the final stage of the climb, then falls at an average of 1 in 90 crossing Chacewater and Blackwater viaducts east of Chacewater station itself.

Like Penwithers, these wooden viaducts were first modified and finally rebuilt. Chacewater, 99 yards length and 52 feet high, was rebuilt in 1888 as was Blackwater, 132 yards long and 68 feet high. The section between Penwithers Junction and Chacewater was doubled in 1914; one section to Baldhu of just under two miles, opened in February, whilst the remaining section to Chacewater was completed in July that year. Chacewater station is described elsewhere in the chapter on the Newquay branch.

From Chacewater viaduct the line again climbs almost to Scorrier. Averaging 1 in 80 for 1½ miles the line passes the site of the triangular junction once serving the Newquay branch. This enabled trains to and from Newquay to work directly from both the Truro and Redruth directions and is described in the relevant chapter on the branch. Continuing westward, the line eventually descends for a short distance past the former Wheal Busy siding, which once served the famous copper mine nearby and also the site of Hallenbeagle engine house, again an imposing structure from Cornwall's copper producing past. Both these features are on the south side of the line. Mining dominated this landscape and the railway itself is built over the many workings carried on here. The section of line from Chacewater to Scorrier was doubled in December 1902.

Scorrier station was built on an embankment and passing beneath the station at its eastern end was the once important Poldice tramroad dating from the second decade of the nineteenth century. The line linked the rich copper producing district inland around Carharrack and St Day with the seaport of Portreath on the north coast.

From Scorrier the main line fell and climbed in a succession of short sections eventually reaching the summit immediately east of Drump Lane goods yard, Redruth. As at Doublebois, between Liskeard and Bodmin Road, the other summit of the Cornish main line, the route fell away westward down to sea level involving a long climb for eastbound trains, even harsher than that faced in the opposite direction. Apart from its geographical position, the section of line between Scorrier and Redruth is also

A once familiar sight, now no more. A 'Hall' class heads westward with a mixed freight in May 1959. The train is completing the long haul westward from Truro running towards Chacewater. Gradients of 1 in 71 and 1 in 80 for long stretches made this section to the summit extremely hard work. Note the curvature of the line running on to Chacewater and the engine house of the former North Downs Mine on the sky-line and, below it, in the valley, Blackwater viaduct and Chacewater station.
M. Mensing

According to the description accompanying the photograph, the 'down' 'Cornishman', seen here early this century, is passing Chacewater at 60 mph. In fact, the GWR imposed a speed limit of 40 mph and even today, with much improved conditions, the limit stands at 50 mph. Steam rail-motor No. 70 stands in the 'down' sidings whilst railway staff in front of the tank engine have obviously spotted something of concern. The 'down' side accommodation at Chacewater was rebuilt as late as 1955, but nine years later, in October 1964, the station closed completely. *Royal Institution of Cornwall*

Almost the same view, but half a century later 'Castle' class No. 4095 *Harlech Castle* passes Chacewater with the 6.20 p.m. Penzance-Kensington Milk train. The branch platform for Newquay can be seen beyond the train together with the single line route alongside the main line to Blackwater Junction. This view was recorded on 16th May 1959. *M. Mensing*

of interest historically. It comprised the last piece of line to be doubled through the county, this taking place as late as April 1930. (Scorrier – Drump Lane.)

Drump Lane goods depot on the south side of the line, to the east of Redruth station, opened in June 1912 replacing the facilities originally sited at the station itself. Goods traffic at the station yard site transferred to Drump Lane on 17th June, the same day that the new depot opened for business. Drump Lane was an open, spacious, site that reflected the volume of trade passing in and out of the district, adding prestige to the GWR and to the town. The West of England Bacon Curing Company was established at Redruth in 1892 providing very useful traffic by rail. This company, opposite Drump Lane goods shed, on the north side of the line, was bought by C.&T. Harris Ltd. of Calne in 1900 and private sidings to deal with their traffic were in operation in the years before World War One. Drump Lane signalbox on the 'up', north, side of the line controlled all movements relating to the goods yard and private sidings.

Prior to the doubling of the line between Drump Lane and Redruth station, a siding ran through the short tunnel at the east end of the station and alongside Tunnel Terrace. It terminated just short of Drump Road and adjacent to the 'Cathedral Boot Works' running beside the main line on the alignment of what was to become the 'down' main line when doubling took place in December 1911.

Redruth's links with railways date back to the late 1820s long before the arrival of the West Cornwall line in 1852. The Redruth and Chacewater Railway, an important 4 foot gauge mineral line, was extended to the town in 1827. This railway linked the rich copper mining district of Gwennap with the river port of Devoran to the south and was officially opened in January 1826. It closed to traffic in 1915 but the northern terminus at Redruth to the east of the present day station can still be located. The site is clearly marked by the alignment of stone sleepers preserved in situ on the south side of St Day Road.

The Hayle Railway also made Redruth its eastern terminus. It occupied a completely different site from that chosen by the later West Cornwall Company, being located a short distance to the west close to the Redruth – Camborne road. Freight traffic between Hayle and Redruth began in June 1838 and a regular passenger service commenced in May 1843. The West Cornwall Company incorporated much of the Hayle Railway, extending and rebuilding it to form part of the overall route from Truro to Penzance. (See GWR in West Cornwall.)

With Redruth now a through station the original terminus from the Hayle Railway became a goods/coal depot on a short branch from Redruth Junction. The Tresavean branch which also served an important mining district south-west of Redruth, likewise left the main line at Redruth Junction, immediately opposite the old route to the terminus. (See plan.) Redruth Junction itself was controlled by a signalbox on the north side of the main line, the entire site being in a cutting half a mile west of the present day station.

No. 6845 *Paviland Grange* crosses Blackwater viaduct immediately east of Chacewater station on 16th May 1959. The train is an early evening stopping service from Plymouth to Penzance. *M. Mensing*

The stations on the West Cornwall line, most certainly including that at Redruth, came in for much criticism by the mid/late 1870s. In a letter to *The West Briton* in January 1878 a correspondent offered the following description of facilities overall.

> 'Waiting rooms where they exist (are) little better than dungeons . . . furniture more ruined and rude than that of a backwood cabin, carpets or floor covers more ragged than those of a fifth-rate lodging house, walls defiled with obscene inscriptions or blastphemies, timetables fingered into obscurity, fire places either cold or rusty or pouring volumes of smoke and blacks.'

The correspondent continued by describing such premises as 'dens, loathsome even to decent artisans'. He also criticised the lack of footbridges and the danger that came from crossing the actual line itself.

Redruth was one of the three crossing places on the West Cornwall line, Camborne and Hayle being the others. No foot-

Redruth, looking westward, before the introduction of mixed gauge in November 1866. The timber viaduct is well illustrated here together with the early station buildings. Carn Brea, with its monument and castle, dominates the background, whilst mining interests can be seen at the foot of the hill beyond the station. *Cornwall County Museum*

A view from a similar vantage point shows the line is laid to mixed gauge and the viaduct is still the original timber structure, not being rebuilt until 1888 when an imposing masonry construction replaced it. The goods shed is far more spacious than the diminutive accommodation for passengers. *Redruth Local Studies Library*

Redruth seen here earlier this century. The goods yard is on the 'down' side with the signalbox at the east end of the station. Considerable improvements took place here principally in 1932 when the station was rebuilt. The footbridge was provided in 1888. Carn Brea Hill dominates to the west with its distinctive monument and castle alongside. *Redruth Local Studies Library*

Redruth, looking westward in 1909. The Territorials are seen here assembled on the 'up' platform as their train arrives from Penzance. A sizeable crowd has gathered to witness their departure, making something of an occasion locally. Such scenes were to become all too familiar soon afterwards with the outbreak of World War One. Redruth's 'up' platform also saw large gatherings of unemployed miners through the late nineteenth and early twentieth centuries when, with their families, they began leaving the area as emigrants. *Cornwall County Museum*

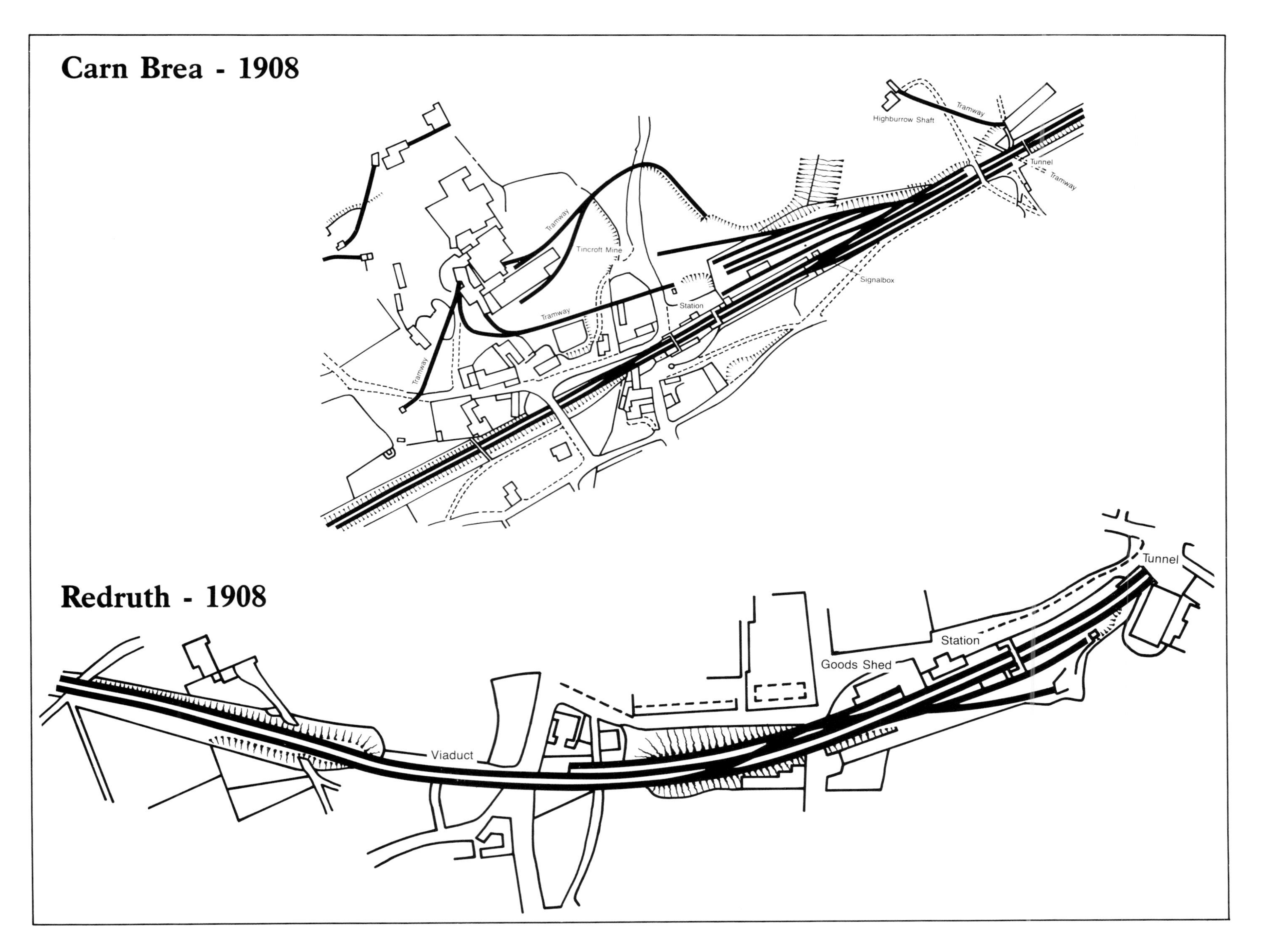
Carn Brea - 1908
Highburrow Shaft
Tramway
Tunnel
Tramway
Tramway
Tincroft Mine
Signalbox
Station
Tramway
Tramway
Redruth - 1908
Tunnel
Station
Goods Shed
Viaduct

The 1 in 15 incline on the Tresavean branch. A maximum of four loaded wagons were allowed on the wire-worked incline with the ascending traffic counterbalancing those on the descent. Locomotives climbed the half-mile incline light engine. The branch closed on 1st January 1936, Tresavean Mine closing earlier, in August 1928. Photograph dated 1934, B.Y. Williams. *Cornwall County Museum*

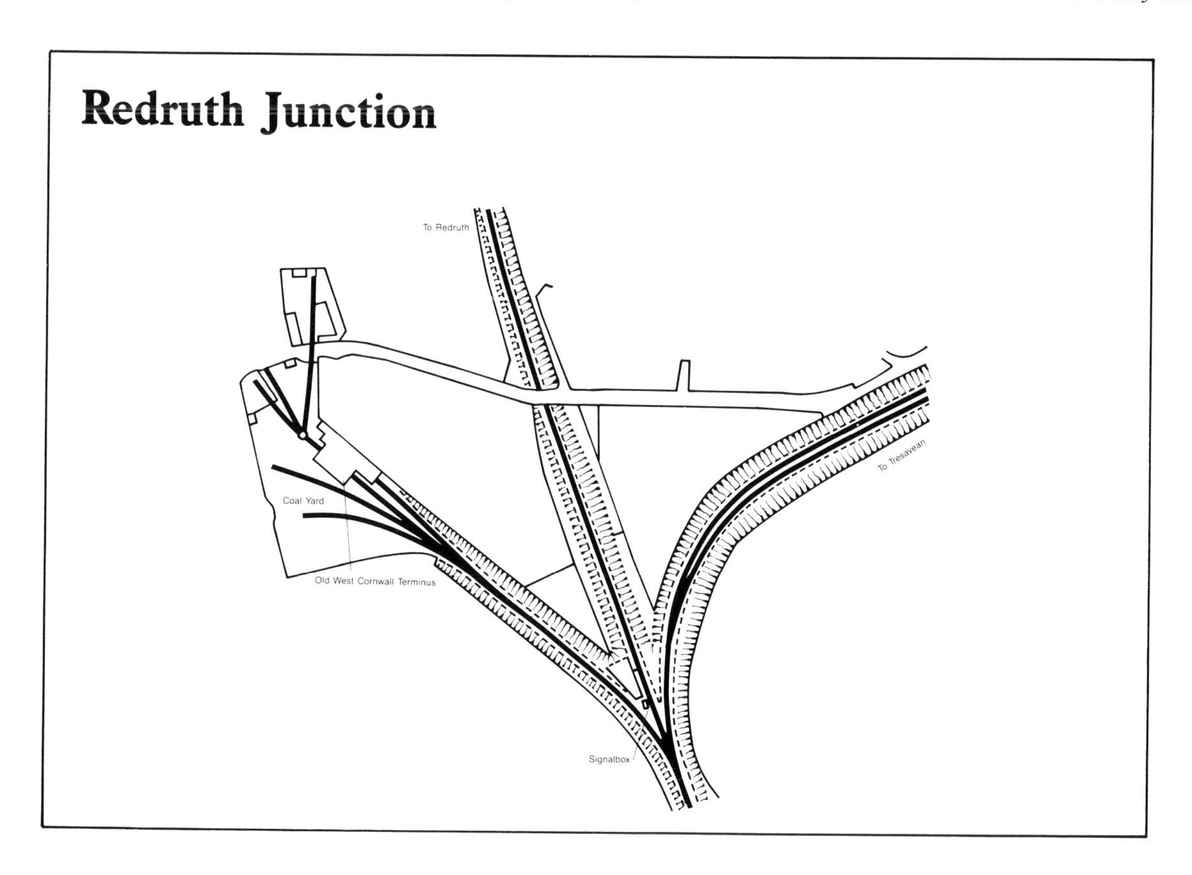

Carn Brea station set in the midst of an important tin and copper producing district. This view looking westward from the 'up' platform shows the presence of the many engine houses serving the mines on both sides of the line. East of the station on the 'up' side there was an extensive yard and the site of the former works of the West Cornwall Railway. Carn Brea station closed in 1961. *Redruth Local Studies Library*

bridges were provided by 1878 and at Redruth, as at Penzance, goods accommodation was far more generous and imposing than that offered passengers. Improvements had followed by 1908 as the plan for that year shows. It also indicates the presence and position of the Redruth and Chacewater terminus slightly to the east. From comparisons with earlier maps, the 1908 plan shows that much of the area reaching southward between these two railways came in for considerable development from the late Victorian period onward. A great deal of quality housing and the provision of the Victoria Park itself, (1897) replaced an area of open ground and the site of the former 'Stamps' workings for breaking ore from Pednandrea Mine nearby. Such obvious improvements as a public park and valuable housing reflected growing affluence and a concern for the image of the town despite the downward fortunes of mining locally.

The GWR opened its new goods depot at Drump Lane in 1912 and twenty years later rebuilt the passenger accommodation at the station. These were welcome improvements but they came too late for many of the local people to benefit. Copper mining had collapsed in the 1860s; so too did tin mining in the early twentieth century. Large numbers of miners had left or were leaving the district, whilst the onset of widespread unemployment in the inter-war years saw further considerable suffering for an area wedded to mining and engineering generally. Tin mining was so badly hit that emergency relief bodies were established locally to help take the edge off the hardship. Emigration was at least a realistic option and the 'up' platform at Redruth was the scene of much activity. Large numbers of unemployed workers gathered there joining special trains taking them and their families eastward to other parts of Britain or, more often, overseas.

Population figures reflect the process of decline at Redruth linked to the steadily increasing problems for mining.

1911 – 10,814
1921 – 9,920
1931 – 9,904
1951 – 9,704

The population of the Redruth – Camborne urban district during the period 1931-1939 declined by 4.3 per thousand per annum.

Carn Brea station, just over midway between Redruth and Camborne, and otherwise known as Pool, (pre 1875) was literally surrounded by mining setts. Many shafts and tunnels were worked alongside and beneath the line. Immediately to the north of the station was Tincroft Mine and to the south towards the slopes of Carn Brea was Carn Brea Mine itself. East of the station and

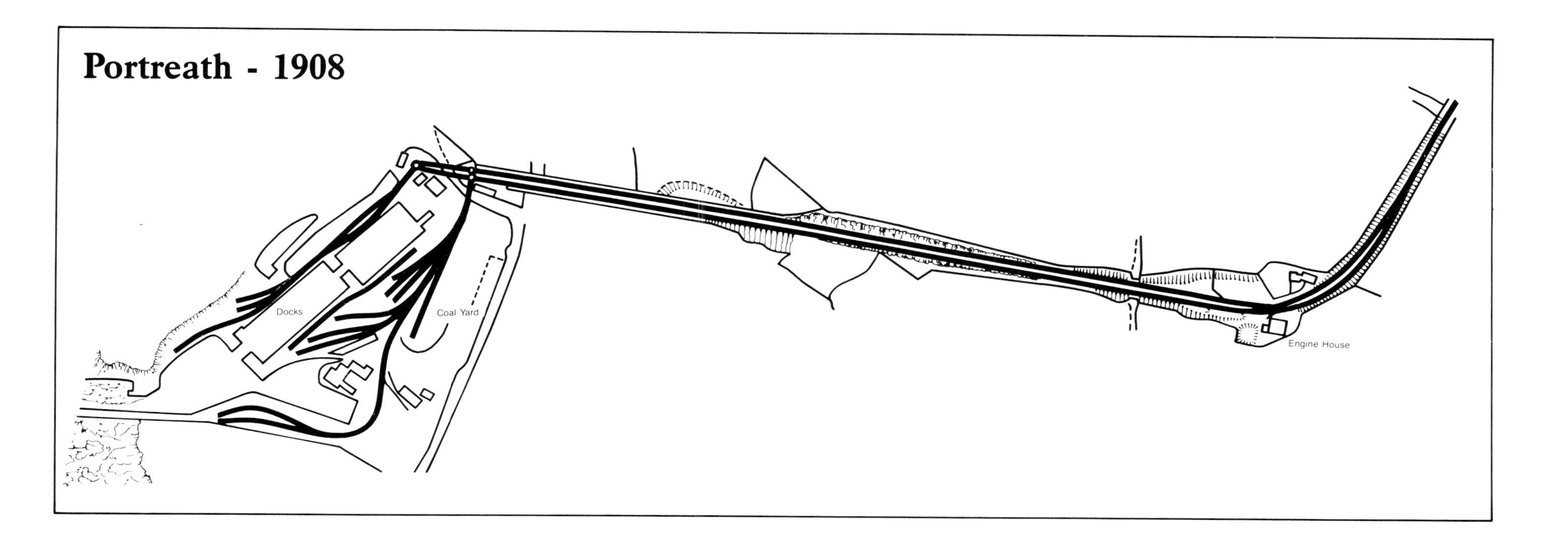

Two views showing features of the Portreath Incline. This 1 in 7 gradient was built for double track and was worked by a stationary engine raising or lowering wagons by wire rope. The photographs show the engine house with its water tank at the head of the incline, and the incline itself reaching down into Portreath, where it crossed the road en route to the harbour.

Cornwall County Museum

Nos. 7812 *Erlestoke Manor* and 6825 *Llanvair Grange* head eastward through Camborne with the 11.10 am SO, Penzance – Wolverhampton on 18th July 1959. Note the extra coaches added to the weekday stock of 'The Cornishman', and the 1 in 67 gradient beyond the station. The 'down' platform was shorter than that on the 'up' side, in order to give access to the goods yard. '5700' class 0-6-0 No. 3702, can be seen here alongside the goods shed, whilst shunting the yard. Truro locomotive depot, 83F, worked the pick-up freights westward to Camborne, with this particular locomotive, No. 3702, being a very regular performer on this turn. An interesting summer weekday service of 1959 was the 7.55 am Camborne – Bristol, arriving Bristol at 1.35 pm. *P. Gray*

its yard was the original site of the West Cornwall Railway Workshops, on ground north of the line and west of the junction for the Portreath branch. The plan of Carn Brea station and surrounding area (1908) shows the layout of the station and its yard. This district was also famous for being the birthplace of the great engineer Richard Trevithick (1771-1833) born in a cottage at Pool nearby.

The Redruth – Camborne district has long held an enviable reputation for its numerous quality engineering establishments, many of them originating from services to mining generally. The industrial nature of the landscape and economy within this district makes for interesting comparisons and contrasts, particularly with the more rural areas eastward, beyond Truro, and westward beyond Camborne. With its heavy commitment to mining and engineering it was inevitable that the area would attract railway development at an early stage. Unlike the china clay district further east, however, the great years for production and profit occurred before the arrival of the Great Western Railway, but even when the company had established itself locally its direct impact on mining interests was limited.

Chapter Four

The Falmouth Branch

The Falmouth line opened to traffic on 24th August 1863, seventeen years after the original Act of Incorporation. Under the Act of 3rd August 1846, the Cornwall Railway was to run from Plymouth to Falmouth providing an invaluable link between the two ports. There was clearly great support for the line at Falmouth and considerable disappointment also when the widespread financial crisis of 1847 imposed economies and delays in construction. The result was that only a single line between Plymouth and Truro opened to traffic in May 1859. All proposals for branches to Bodmin, Newham (Truro) and Penryn quays together with the intended connection with the Liskeard and Caradon Company were abandoned, whilst work on the Falmouth line itself during the early 1850s was brought to a halt. Only after much protest and, in the meantime, the opening of the new docks at Falmouth was work resumed. A consolidating Act of 1861 enabled this work to go ahead to completion, four years after the initial opening from Plymouth to Truro. With the endless delays now behind them – 'the long desert filled with fears, disappointments and snubbings' – the people of Falmouth and the communities along the line looked to a great new era of good fortune. According to the local press, Falmouth was 'no longer the land of promise cut off from the millions . . .'

The line, 11¾ miles long, was built to the broad gauge under the direction of Brunel's former Chief Assistant, R.P. Brereton. Heavy engineering was required with the need for two tunnels, eight viaducts and extensive earthworks generally. Messrs Sharpe and Sons were awarded the contract, initially, for the section from Truro to Penryn and, thereafter, that from Penryn to Falmouth. Construction costs were given as £172,000, excluding the price of land and station buildings. Olver and Sons of Falmouth, highly regarded local contractors, were responsible for station buildings on the line; Perran, which later became Perranwell, Penryn and Falmouth itself. With the opening of Falmouth docks it was also decided not to carry the line to Greenbank nearer the centre of the town as originally intended, but to carry it along the high ground beyond Penryn and west of Falmouth to the dockside site for easy interchange of traffic. The connection to the docks opened in January 1864.

At the opposite end of the line, Truro became much busier with the new additional services. On leaving the station the broad gauge Cornwall Railway line ran westward parallel with the standard gauge West Cornwall line to Penzance. Climbing on a 1 in 60 gradient through Highertown tunnel the two routes parted company at Penwithers, where, also, the West Cornwall Railway Company's line to Newham Wharf cut across the Falmouth route. The Cornwall Railway route to Falmouth followed a straight alignment from Highertown towards Penwithers viaduct whilst the West Cornwall route curved away westward to Redruth and Penzance. The original 'main line' status of the line to Falmouth was clearly indicated in this arrangement.

Penwithers viaduct, a timber structure resting on masonry piers, was only a short distance beyond what later became Penwithers Junction. The viaduct was 271 yards long and 90 feet high and was to be replaced in October 1926, by an embankment. The gradient along this section is a 1 in 66 ascent extending for approximately a mile. Penwithers Cutting, beyond the viaduct, runs for some 924 feet leading then to a slight ease of gradient a short distance east of Sparnick tunnel.

Like Perran tunnel, the other on the line, Sparnick was cut through shale and slate and lined with masonry throughout. The tunnel is 491 yards long and is built on a falling gradient of 1 in 88; thereafter the line falls more steeply at an average of 1 in 64. Ringwell viaduct was the next structure to follow. At 122 yards in length and 70 feet high, it was one of three to be replaced by embankments, this one in September 1933.

A little over half a mile before Perranwell station, the line crosses Carnon viaduct. This was 252 yards long at a height of 96 feet. The 4-foot gauge Redruth and Chacewater mineral line passed beneath it, running along the river's east bank, linking the Gwennap copper producing district with the river port of Devoran. Carnon posed problems in construction, mainly with the establishment of secure foundations in the sandy river bed. Stabilisation was extremely difficult, but with the use of protective cast iron cylinders and careful pumping the piers were set in place. A new masonry viaduct was brought into use in June 1933.

Perranwell station, standing just short of milepost 305, was a very appealing Cornish country location. The main building was a granite structure with booking and parcels offices, a ladies and general waiting room and conveniences. A verandah also protected the entire width of the platform for the length of the building. A small waiting room and a lamp and coal room was also provided on the opposite platform. Set back from the main building and immediately westward was the stone goods shed 46 feet long and 35 feet wide with a small office set into the west wall. Alongside the goods shed was an excellent elevated signalbox set at right angles to the line; straddling the 'down' siding between the goods shed and the platforms.

Almost a mile beyond Perranwell came Perran viaduct. This was 113 yards long and 56 feet high, being replaced by a masonry structure in April 1927. Here the gradient rises at 1 in 66 but eases back to 1 in 100 at Perran Tunnel, 404 yards long. Cut through abounding slate and shale it needed lining throughout. Milepost 306½ marks its southern end, the line having curved round to a north-south alignment after Perranwell. A heavy climb follows soon after at 1 in 60 for upwards of a mile leading to Ponsanooth viaduct where the line curves again taking a south easterly course.

Ponsanooth was 215 yards long and 139 feet high making it the fourth highest viaduct in Cornwall and the highest of the viaducts on the Falmouth line itself. It was replaced by a masonry

'4575' class 2-6-2 No. 5533 waits to leave Truro from the Falmouth bay platform with the 5.15 pm service to the terminus. 15th May 1959. An overall speed limit of 50 mph was imposed on the branch, but speed over many sections of the line was well below this top limit. Journey time was generally 30 minutes for the 11¾ miles. *M. Mensing*

Ringwell viaduct as photographed in the 1920s with a '4500' class 2-6-2T crossing with a freight train. This viaduct was one of four on the branch replaced by embankments. Ringwell, between Sparnick tunnel and Carnon viaduct, was replaced in 1933, with the new embankment opening to traffic on 17th September. *Cornwall County Museum*

A view of Carnon viaduct in the early years of this century, with a train making for Truro. This timbered structure, standing on the stone piers, lasted until June 1933 when it was replaced by a masonry viaduct. The line running beneath, and alongside the river, was the 4 foot gauge Redruth and Chacewater Railway built to link the copper mining district inland with the port of Devoran. This railway closed in 1917; happily the Falmouth branch is still in business. *Redruth Local Studies Library*

A long and mixed freight working approaches Penwithers Junction from Falmouth on 16th May 1959. Headed by a single '4500' class tank, the train is passing over the site of the former Penwithers viaduct which was replaced by an embankment in October 1926. *P.Q. Treloar*

structure in 1930. Just over a quarter of a mile further was Pascoe viaduct, 130 yards long and 70 feet high; it was replaced by an embankment in August 1923. The deepest cutting on the entire line follows soon after; known as Roskrow Hill, it was cut through elvan in certain places and required the removal of 100,000 cubic yards of soil. The line then continues its descent towards Penryn on a 1 in 60 gradient overall crossing beneath the now classified A 39 road from Truro to Falmouth, thence running alongside it for a short distance.

Before entering Penryn station the line crossed Penryn viaduct, 114 yards long and 83 feet high. This was replaced by an embankment and also entailed a realignment of the track with the effect that Penryn station was also rebuilt slightly to the west of the original site. Whereas the original station was built on a slight curve, the new line of 1923 was on a straight section. Accommodation for the new arrangement was not as generous as that for the old but the facilities as originally provided were maintained in the old station building. The latter, a large granite structure, included booking office, parcels office, ladies and general waiting rooms and, of course, conveniences. The station building was situated on the 'down' east side of the line, as was the goods shed.

Penryn's goods shed was larger than that at Perranwell, being 67 feet by 45 feet wide. Two cranes were provided to handle the substantial traffic passing through the yard. Unlike today, Penryn was a very busy, important location during the second half of the nineteenth century. In August 1869 *The West Briton* commented upon trade at the town:

> 'Its ten steam engines have been constantly at work, employing a large number of hands. The granite trade has been very brisk, the workmen earning from 5 shillings to 6 shillings a day, each with full employment. The cattle trade has been steady throughout the year, upwards of 2,500 head have been imported. The iron foundry has been constantly at work, employing a great number of hands. The paper mills of Mr Mead are also doing a large amount of business . . . Tanyards (providing good rail trade to Bristol) coal stores, lime kilns and flour mills also place the town commercially in a very healthy state'.

The railway inevitably took a good share in the prosperity of Penryn. A double approach road was provided to the station, one giving direct access to traffic from Helston, Stithians and Ponsanooth, the other serving Penryn itself and the communities of the Budock and Constantine districts. A signalbox was also provided on the 'down' platform of the original station and, likewise, one was also installed at the Falmouth end of the 'new' station on the 'down' side.

From Penryn the line falls away steeply towards College Wood viaduct reaching gradients of 1 in 51. College Wood was a quarter of a mile beyond Penryn station, the viaduct being 318 yards long and 100 feet high. It was notable for being the longest on the Falmouth line and for being the last of the timber structures to remain in operation. It was replaced in July 1934. As the line curves to the east on College Wood viaduct it offers excellent views of Penryn and the waterfront. The rising gradient on the embankment beyond the viaduct was the scene of a serious accident on 31st October 1898. The 5.20 pm 'Mail' train from Falmouth was derailed on the embankment, and after tearing out a length of track the locomotive crashed down the slope into the field below, burrowing itself into the soil. Only the leading vehicle, the mail coach, was thrown over onto its side and the two passenger coaches remained upright. Whilst the passengers avoided serious physical injury the driver, Mr Cotterill, subsequently died from severe scalding.

With the decision to take the line to the docks and not to Greenbank as originally intended under the 1846 Act, the line followed a south easterly course keeping to the higher ground west of Falmouth itself. An additional 'station' in the shape of Penmere Platform was later opened on this section of the line in July 1925 to serve the growing community to the west of the town, this being close to milepost 311¼. MOD sidings for oil traffic were also opened on the west side of the line immediately beyond Penmere Platform in 1940. A steep descent at 1 in 80, a curve eastward and a succession of cuttings and embankments brought the line to the terminus overlooking the docks yet at the same time distancing itself from the centre of the town.

Collegewood viaduct old and new. This view, looking towards Falmouth, shows the new masonry viaduct opened in July 1934 alongside the original structure dating back to the opening of the line in 1863. Collegewood was the last of the timber viaducts to be replaced in Cornwall. Note the modification to the far embankment, required through realignment of the track. *Royal Institution of Cornwall*

The terminus was intended to impress. It was an imposing site incorporating the terminal building itself, a goods shed and yard and a locomotive depot with turntable. The main station building was 200 feet long and 90 feet wide with an overall roof taking in a span of 70 feet. Separate arrival and departure platforms were provided with a third line for storing coaching stock between them. The station front faced south and included a large verandah, a central booking office, first, second and ladies waiting rooms along with a parcels office and conveniences. The building was constructed in dressed granite.

The goods yard and wooden shed were on the 'up' south side of the line. Three cranes were provided, the shed itself being 100 feet long and 61 feet wide. A turntable for rolling stock was also installed between the station area and the goods yard. West of the station and on the 'up' side was the signalbox, and beyond this again was the locomotive depot, a stone structure with two roads. Originally the turntable was just east of the shed but at the turn of the century it was replaced by another, this time to the rear of the buildings.

On the north side of the line was the link to the docks. *The West Briton* covered the opening of this important section enabling the Falmouth Docks Company to enjoy direct access on and off the Cornwall Railway. In this extract dated Friday 15th January 1864 the newspaper related:

> 'The deep cutting from the Cornwall Railway Station at Falmouth to the docks has been completed, and the rails laid thus affording direct railway communication to the docks. On Thursday last an engine belonging to the Cornwall Railway ran for the first time direct to the breakwater at the docks, and a cargo of china clay is expected shortly to be despatched over the Cornwall Railway for shipment on a vessel at the docks.'

Great things were expected from a working partnership between railway and docks. It was hoped that business would boom; that Falmouth would develop as an important commercial port and, with the cooperation of the railway, look to regain its former status as a 'packet' station, lost to Southampton in 1850. Packet status was denied it, however, despite the optimistic forecasts of local interests and efforts on their behalf. In the early eighteenth century Daniel Defoe described Falmouth as 'certainly next to Milford Haven in South Wales, the fairest and best road for shipping that is in the whole of Britain'. He considered the town 'well built' with an 'abundance of shipping belonging to it, is full of rich merchants, and has a flourishing and increasing trade'.

Business interests of the 1860s were clearly mindful of Falmouth's illustrious past intending that their vast expanse of sheltered deep water should be put to best use. The newly opened graving docks enhanced Falmouth's status for ship repair whilst the construction of new wharfs and breakwaters on the part of the Docks Company encouraged trade and, with it, Falmouth's reputation for coastal and international shipping. By 1866 nine steam tugs were reported at work and substantial imports of timber, wheat and livestock were noted. The first consignment of china clay by rail came in January 1864 when ten wagons carrying almost 100 tons arrived from Burngullow sent by the West of England China Clay Company.

No. 5500 arrives at Falmouth with the 10.50 am ex Newquay, the 12.03 pm ex Truro on Sunday 17th May 1959. Through workings between Newquay and Falmouth were quite common on Sundays at that time, providing a useful opportunity for tourists to travel from the north to south coast and vice-versa with ease. Falmouth station, although deprived of its overall roof, was in remarkably good condition in 1959. The goods yard was still in demand, but the locomotive shed had closed many years before, in the early 1920s. *M. Mensing*

With the development of the deep water harbour at Fowey, by the Cornwall Minerals Railway in 1874, china clay exports were concentrated there. Falmouth, however, or specifically the River Fal, again became the facus of interest in the early years of this century. The St Just Ocean Wharves and Railway intended to build a line from the clay producing district of Mid Cornwall to the deep waters of St Just Pool on the east shore of the Fal. The scheme did not make great headway in the harsh financial climate following World War One, but the project again attracted publicity in 1924. Both the Great Western Railway and the Falmouth Docks Company registered strong opposition, with the idea eventually falling through. The intention to strike south-westward to the Fal was originally the idea of W.R. Roebuck whose early initiative with the Cornwall Minerals Company included proposals for a line extending down the Fal Valley from Meledor Mill, in the 1870s.

The arrival of the Railway also enabled Falmouth and the surrounding area to flourish as a fashionable centre for tourism. A genial climate, the outstanding natural beauty of the Fal and Helford Rivers, the coastal scenery and discreet charms of the Roseland Peninsula could not fail to attract the eager traveller.

On the question of climate the Physician in Ordinary to Queen Victoria herself, Sir Edward Sieveking, wrote a paper on Falmouth as a holiday resort. Of the location he recorded:

> 'Here we have at our doors a health resort abounding in beauty and loveliness, rich in health-giving properties: and if we but use our opportunities, I have little doubt generations to come will attribute to Falmouth, a restoration to health and a renewal of life.'

The Great Western Railway was only too pleased to be able to include such testimony in its famous publication *The Cornish Riviera* and indeed, went on to describe Falmouth as that particular place where: 'The climate is that of the lotus-eaters'. The Company also considered Falmouth to be worthy of comparison with locations described in Greek verse, as in Virgil's 'OEnid'. Nearer to home and to their own day, the Company also quoted Lord Rosebury who called upon Falmouth to 'preserve your beauty, for you will need it in the days to come, for the visitors who will throng to you'.

Falmouth took itself seriously as a potential resort. In May 1865 the Falmouth Hotel opened to business offering prestigious accommodation in a magnificent setting close to the sea, overlooking the river, the estuary and the bay. Slightly earlier that same year, a new carriageway was opened to the public offering them access around the headland below Pendennis Castle, previously under the exclusive ownership of the War Office. 1865 also saw proposals for 'a limited liability company – for the purpose of providing a bathing establishment at Gyllyngvase beach'.

When the railway opened in 1863, however, many were aware that if tourism was to develop and Falmouth take the identity of a fashionable watering place, a great deal of effort was required in the provision of public amenities. During November 1863, therefore, powers were sought to form a Local Board to implement improvements covering 'paving, lighting, drainage, cleansing and otherwise regulating and improving the district. To contract for supply of water, supply of gas, construction of sewers, regulate formation of streets and the construction of buildings'. The more informed sources of public opinion recognised that with important new development such as railway links and the new docks came opportunities that must not be put at risk by unimaginative local leadership. this much was stated openly by civil leaders.

The guide book to Falmouth for 1877 emphasised that all the necessary arrangements for the provision of bathing machines at Gyllyngvase Beach had been made. Ladies and children had the eastern side of the beach reserved for them; gentlemen used the western side. Plans were also pursued to obtain public control of the beach and its immediate environment and to create

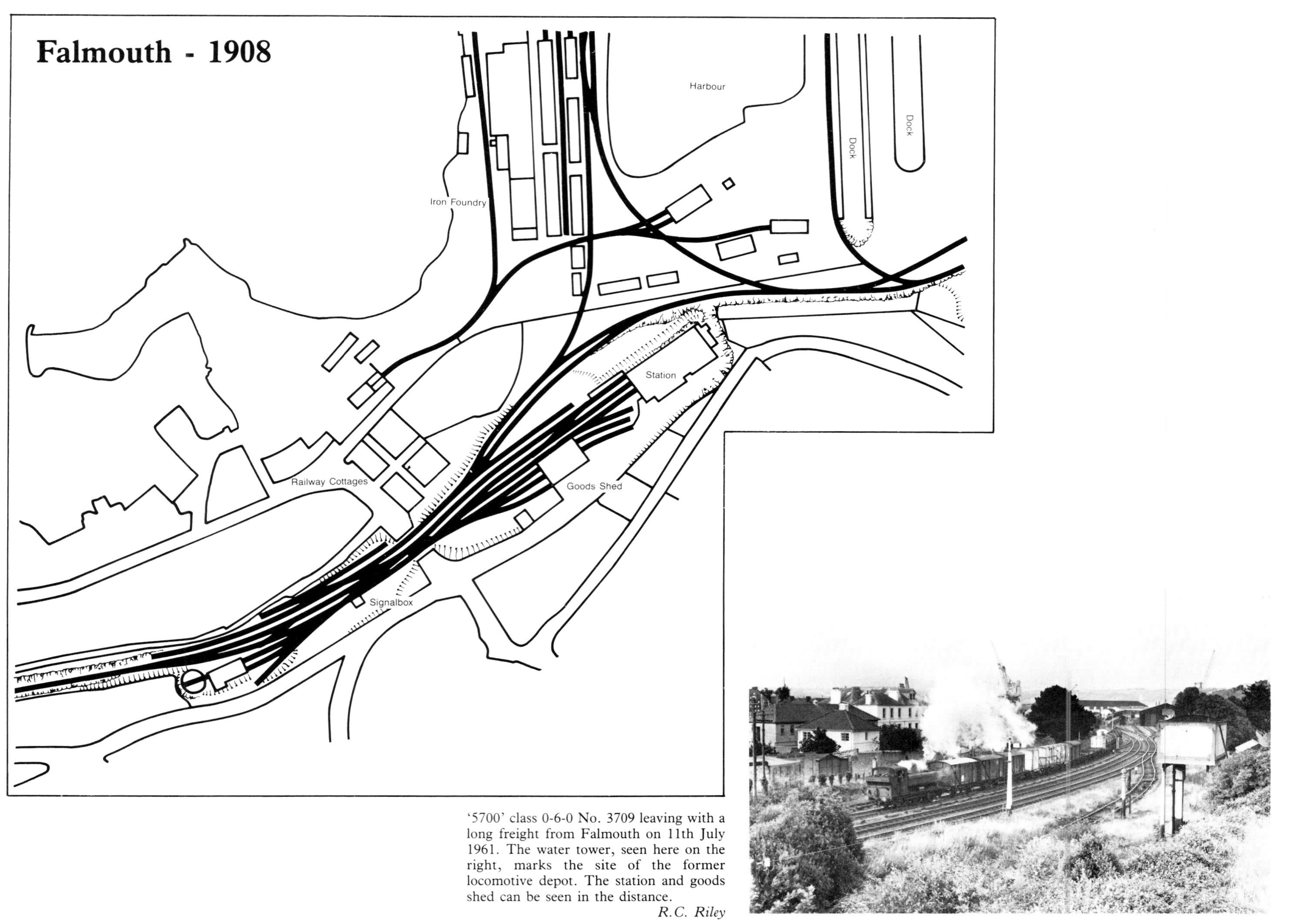

'5700' class 0-6-0 No. 3709 leaving with a long freight from Falmouth on 11th July 1961. The water tower, seen here on the right, marks the site of the former locomotive depot. The station and goods shed can be seen in the distance.

R.C. Riley

'4500' class tank No. 4574 shunts the yard at Falmouth. Beyond is the massive, but imposing, Falmouth Hotel opened in May 1865, underlining the fact that Falmouth also had serious ambitions as a resort as well as being an important port. Freight traffic to and from this great deep water harbour was never as intensive as was hoped for. Considerable trade was carried on in the earlier years, hence the size of the yard and the importance of direct rail links with the docks. In the twentieth century, however, Falmouth became primarily a ship-repair centre and not the trading port anticipated, as in the case of Southampton. 15th May 1959. *M. Mensing*

attractions such as an ornamental gardens. The marshland at Gyllyngvase was also marked for drainage and development. With final reference to the 1870s it is worth noting that in 1875 Thomas Cook's rapidly expanding interests in the travel market devoted time to Falmouth and its surrounding area. Together with officials from the Midland Railway, Thomas Cook anticipated a tour covering the district for the coming 1876 season.

By the early years of the present century, a pleasure ground, winter gardens and Queen Mary Gardens were further attractions to tourists along the sea front area. A promenade was also made a valuable feature adding to the overall effect of a dignified resort. During the inter-war years Falmouth also responded enthusiastically to the development of the 'Come to Cornwall Association', formed to promote tourism collectively within the county. The GWR's combined rail-rover, and area run-about tickets proved very popular, also particularly as at that time Cornwall's rail network gave easy access to all parts of the county.

With reference to train services, the line opened officially on 21st August 1863, normal service beginning three days later on 24th August. The official train was drawn by the locomotives *Antelope* and *Wolf*, its arrival at Falmouth signalling great festivities, not least for the extensive delays on the part of the Cornwall Railway in opening to the town. By October 1863 the timetable offered five trains in each direction serving destinations outside the county. Through summer workings were a feature of the line between the two World Wars, returning again after World War Two with summer Saturday services during the 1950s linking Paddington and Bristol. On weekdays in summer timetable there was also a through train to Paddington, with a corresponding service westward. By the closing years of the 1960s only one through working to Paddington remained, leaving Falmouth at 09.26. An overall speed limit of 50 mph was imposed on the branch.

By this time also, the branch was long past its best and subject to the inevitable process of economies and cuts. Falmouth station itself was closed in December 1970 to be replaced by a new halt named 'The Dell' a half a mile or so from the old terminus, but much nearer the town centre. By any standards this was a marked decline, but it was a feature reflected all along the line. Perranwell closed to goods on 4th January 1965, and just over a year later all facilities other than the original 'down' line disappeared. A similar story applied at Penryn but here the process took a little longer to complete. Fortunately the terminus was reopened in 1975 and once more through workings returned. Such luxuries ceased with the ending of the summer season of 1979, the last remaining working being the 09.10 departure to Paddington. Under the 1984-85 timetable 11 trains ran in each direction on weekdays with one extra service provided on Saturdays in summer. The line is now signalled at Penwithers Junction alone, controlling movements on and off the branch. All stations are now no more than unstaffed halts, but at Falmouth the decline is most apparent. Shorn of its overall roof, goods shed, signalbox and locomotive depot, the single, solitary platform plays host to DMU services operating on weekdays only. Although built as a single track railway except for passing loops at Perranwell and Penryn and a short double track section at Penwithers Junction, the Cornwall Railway purchased land and built its overbridges to accommodate double track if an when required. Such provision seems both lavish and remote by today's standards although there are echoes of former optimism in the recent discussion concerning Falmouth's development as a container port.

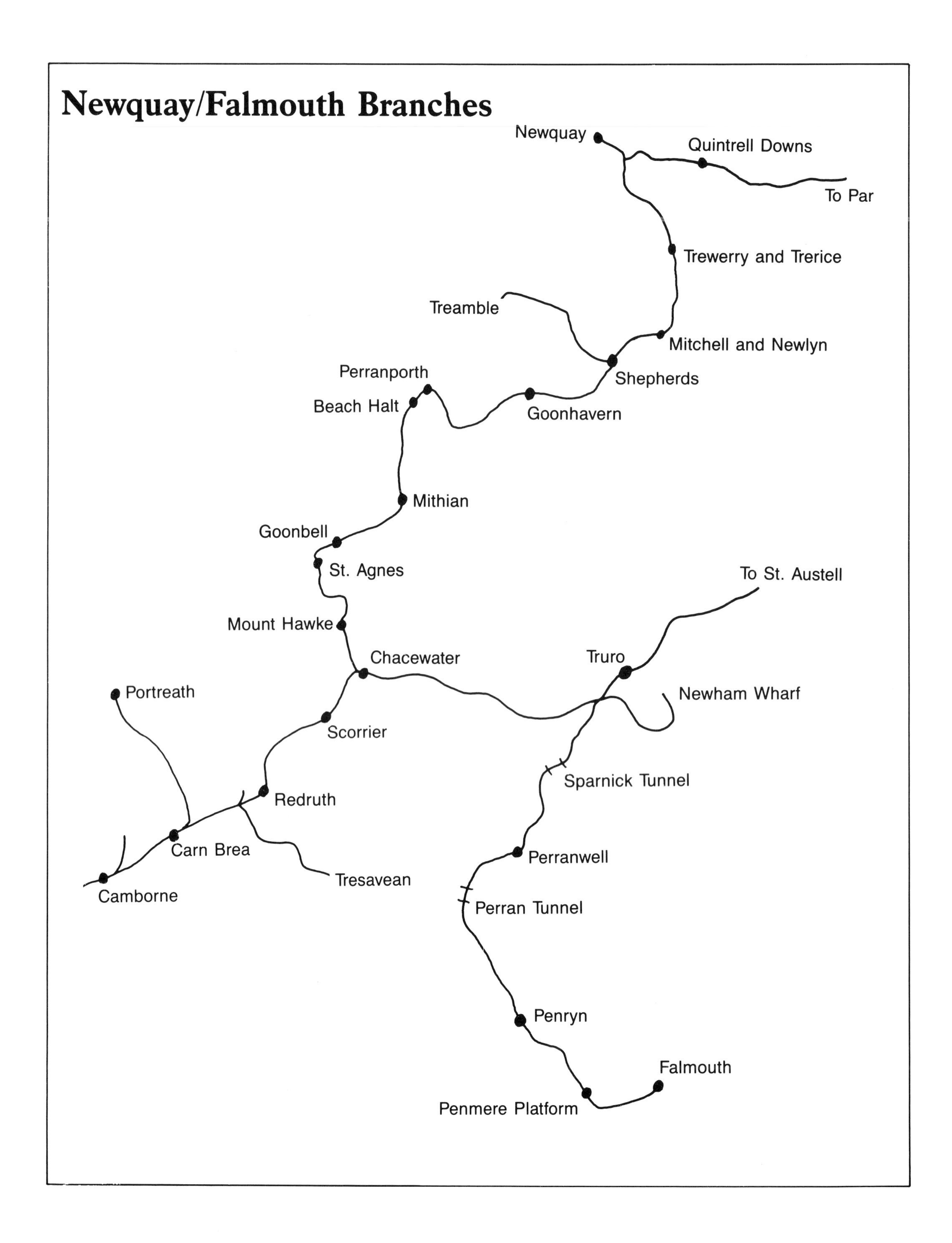

Newquay/Falmouth Branches
Newquay
Quintrell Downs
To Par
Trewerry and Trerice
Treamble
Mitchell and Newlyn
Shepherds
Perranporth
Beach Halt
Goonhavern
Mithian
Goonbell
St. Agnes
To St. Austell
Mount Hawke
Chacewater
Truro
Portreath
Newham Wharf
Scorrier
Sparnick Tunnel
Redruth
Carn Brea
Tresavean
Camborne
Perranwell
Perran Tunnel
Penryn
Falmouth
Penmere Platform

Chapter Five

The Chacewater - Newquay Branch

Together with its more important link via the clay district to Par, Newquay was also host to the branch from Chacewater on the main line 5 miles west of Truro. Total distance over the line was 18½ miles, but it was opened in two separate stages. Chacewater (Blackwater Junction) to Perranporth opened to traffic on 6th July 1903, whilst the section from Perranporth to Newquay (Tolcarne Junction) followed on 2nd January 1905. The latter section also incorporated the earlier CMR branch from Shepherds to Tolcarne with Messrs Rolf and Son of Plymouth carrying out the necessary improvements, upgrading to passenger standards. The contractor between Blackwater Junction and Shepherds was Arthur Carkeek of Redruth; who was also responsible for the three stations – St Agnes, Perranporth and Shepherds. The resident engineer was Mr W.F. Fox who was also in charge of the new line from Saltash to St Germans in East Cornwall.

With the opening of the first section to Perranporth (7 miles 45 chains) it was possible to run through trains in both easterly and westerly directions onto the main line. This was possible because of the triangular junction at Blackwater. The GWR emphasised this feature through the local press, drawing attention to its new services:- Perranporth–Truro, Perranporth – Falmouth, and Perranporth – Camborne/Redruth. Return fares were given as 4 shillings (1st) 2s 6d (2nd) and 2s 3d to Truro; 4s 6d (1st) 2s 10d (2nd) and 2s 5d (3rd) to Camborne, and 7 shillings, (1st) 4s 6d (2nd) and 3s 11d (3rd) to Falmouth. Market tickets were also issued for Truro, Redruth and Camborne: the third class return from Perranporth to Truro, for example, on Wednesdays and Saturdays was 1s 3d. The much improved access, mobility and cheaper travel generally was a great advantage to the area in commercial and social terms and could only be further improved when the line opened throughout to Newquay. Direct passenger services westward off the branch only worked during summer seasons however.

Through services to Newquay from Monday 2nd January 1905 made a great difference to the area; they were further improved on 14th August that year with the provision of six new halts along the line. Although a late arrival in railway terms, the branch was more than welcome. In its report *The West Briton* spoke of the event as marking Newquay's 'second birth', and went on to say that the attention of all the other seaside towns was fastened on the resort. Links were now easily available with Penzance, St Ives, Helston and the Lizard Peninsula, Truro and Falmouth without the costly and time consuming journey via Par. The new ordinary return fare from Newquay to Truro, for example, was 2s 6d as opposed to 6s 8d via Par. All the Cornish resorts stood to gain from an easy interchange of passengers adding to the appeal of the Cornish Riviera overall, but the people of Newquay itself were best pleased. Access to the market towns, particularly Truro, was welcomed but the opportunity for Newquay to grow as a holiday and residential centre was uppermost.

With two lines now serving the town, Newquay expressed its thanks to the railway recognising the benefit as they put it, of having 'caught the eye of the Great Western Railway'. Since the arrival of the CMR some thirty years earlier Newquay had grown rapidly. House and hotel building proceeded at an encouraging pace – the improved rateable value has already been

An excellent view, by Peter Gray, of Chacewater on a wet day in early August 1959. No. 4928 *Gatacre Hall* enters the station with the 4.50 pm Penzance – Manchester, as '4575' class 2-6-2T No. 5515 stands at the branch platform with the 5.58 pm Chacewater – Newquay. Opened throughout on 2nd January 1905, the branch closed on 4th February 1963. *P. Gray*

'4575' class No. 5552 leaves Chacewater from the branch platforms for the five mile journey to Truro. Blackwater viaduct, immediately east of the station, is also seen here. Note the destination-board 'Chacewater' on the Hawksworth corridor coach. *M. Mensing*

noted; service improvements via a gas company (1878) a water company some four years later, and a detailed sanitary programme from 1875 provided the basis for further progress as required. At the time when the new branch was under construction the town was also negotiating for the development of valuable land for Trenance Gardens, later to become a prominent feature of the resort. The service rendered to the many local communities through the halts must also be recognised. The railway's contribution in opening up the somewhat isolated stretch of countryside inland and along the north coast was considerable, adding an essential extra quality to local life. Perranporth, of course, was well suited to develop as a resort in its own right.

Only a decade before the full opening of the line, however, the GWR experienced failure over its proposals to build a more direct line from Truro to Newquay. Parliamentary permission was denied after a spirited campaign by certain local interests on behalf of the London and South Western Railway. Even as late as the mid 1890s there were hopes that this rival company might extend westward beyond Wadebridge, but in the event, the opposition only succeeded in delaying the new line to Newquay. Following a mutual agreement on operating areas, the LSWR did not extend its rails further westward, but Newquay was served by the rival company, by way of road from Wadebridge. Full arrangements for two and three day tours from Newquay to Boscastle and Tintagel by the North Cornwall Coach Company in conjunction with the LSWR were available prior to World War One in 1914, indicating the valuable trade in tourism at Newquay. The GWR also offered special excursion rates over its lines and issued holiday season tickets covering all GWR locations within the county.

Newquay had good reason to thank the Great Western. The company was reported to have spent nearly £30,000 on various improvements to the terminus itself in conjunction with the new branch services and, significantly, the increase of traffic from other parts of Britain. New goods accommodation, a locomotive shed and station development was apparent, whilst a service of five trains in each direction was provided on the Chacewater line using rail-motor services.

Returning directly to the new branch connection, it was inspected by Colonel York on behalf of the Board of Trade four days before opening to traffic, the contractor being congratulated on his work particularly in respect of the viaducts. The GWR decided against any formal opening ceremony but a special saloon carriage was made available to members of the Urban District Council who, in turn, enjoyed a trip to Perranporth to mark the occasion. Newquay shopkeepers also closed their premises and the town celebrated with a holiday. The council and the GWR further agreed to give 400 school children a trip to Perranporth during the afternoon, whilst children from Perranporth were brought to Newquay. The first train of the day was the 7.45 am departure from Truro, arriving Newquay at 8.41 am.

Unlike the proposals for the earlier route from Truro to Newquay, the new line was anything but direct. Although the junction station was at Chacewater, the branch was orientated towards the main line locations at Redruth and to a greater degree, Truro. With the closure of Blackwater West junction to passengers on 18th September 1916 and the end of direct services westward off the branch, Truro became the inevitable focal point for services from both an operative and commercial point of view, as always intended.

Chacewater station was originally opened as part of the West Cornwall Railway on 25th August 1852. Detailed changes had obviously taken place by the time the branch to Perranporth opened in 1903. The main buildings at Chacewater were on the 'down' side of the main line together with the signalbox. Also on that side, south of the line, were two short sidings running in from the west behind the main buildings, serving a small yard. The station approach was also from the south. An island platform connected by a footbridge served the 'up' main line and the branch trains, the latter running in on a short loop. Ladies and general waiting rooms were also provided, along with conveniences, this accommodation being stone built whilst the 'down' side was of wood.

Changes were made to Blackwater's triangular junction from 1916. From September that year, until May 1919, the west curve was worked as freight only, and was closed completely at the latter date. The three signalboxes at the junction closed five years later: the West box in September 1924 and the North and East boxes in November that year. With the closure of the East box the branch was extended eastward from the junction on its own independent line for the half-mile run downhill into the station. To achieve this, the cutting west of the station was widened considerably on the north side of the line. Following a major rebuilding programme on the 'down' side, completed in 1955, the station closed entirely on 5th October 1964. A rail served cement terminal now occupies the small yard on the 'down' side (also now closed) whilst the station buildings act as office accommodation. Nothing, other than rubble, remains of the island platform opposite.

From Blackwater East Junction the branch curved northward on a long and substantial embankment crossing over what

Right: The construction gang working on Blackwater overbridge near Chacewater in 1902. This bridge carried the Newquay branch over what later became the main A30 trunk road. *Royal Institution of Cornwall*

Below: '4575' class 2-6-2T No. 5562, enters Mount Hawke Halt with the 4.35 pm Newquay – Truro working on 10th July 1961. The oil lamps and pagoda shelters were interesting features of the branch, with many of the halts serving widespread and isolated communities. Mount Hawke, like all the other halts on the line, was opened on 16th August 1905. *P. Gray*

Truro-based '5700' tank No. 3709, seen here without its spark-arrestor chimney, leaves St Agnes with the 3.20 pm Newquay–Truro on 10th July 1961. The '5700' tanks were not regulars on the branch, the '4575' class being much more common. An overall speed limit of 40 mph applied on the branch. *P. Gray*

Station staff and others pose for the camera at St Agnes during World War One. The stationmaster, centre, was a Mr Julian; the porter, to the right, being one Percival Trembath. *Royal Institution of Cornwall*

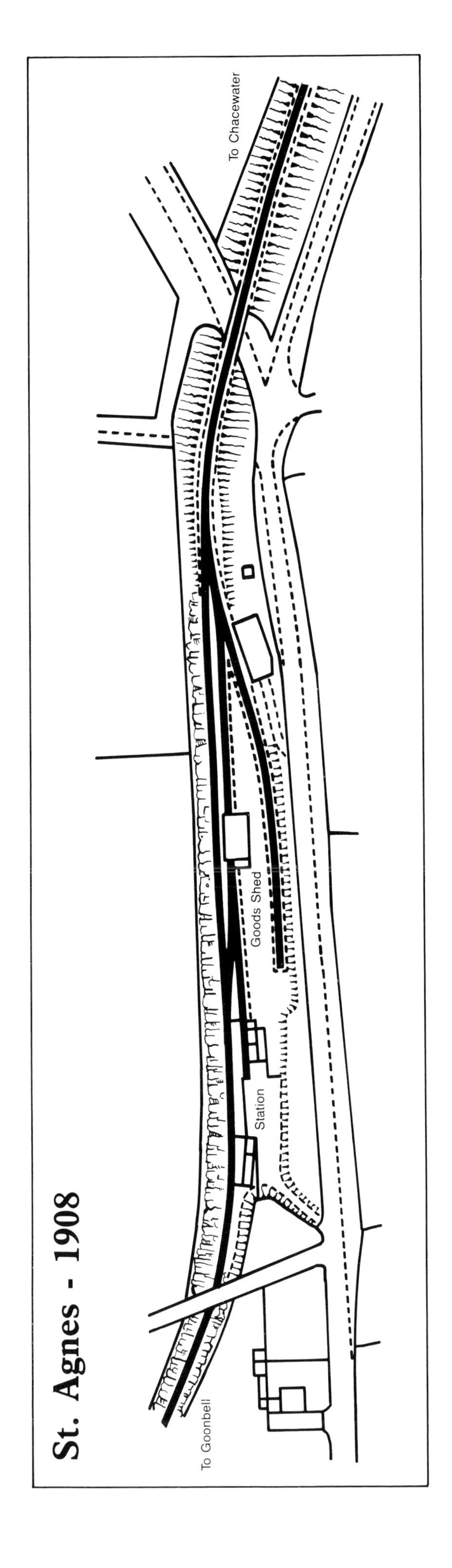

is now the A30 trunk road. Mount Hawke was the first stop from 16th August 1905 when all the original halts were opened. This was a single platform with a pagoda providing shelter, the entire site being located in a cutting. After Mount Hawke the line followed a long curve east, then west eventually continuing northward, climbing along a well-defined embankment to St Agnes, 3¼ miles from Chacewater. In fairly typical style, the station was some way distant from the village itself. St Agnes was originally a single platform on the west side of the line; an essentially Edwardian country station of red brick with a generous awning, oil lamps and numerous enamelled advertisements. In 1937 the station was rebuilt on a much more ambitious scale. A 300-foot island platform was provided, with access by an overbridge at the north end of the platform. The bridge was sharply angled to allow for lack of space, even though the embankment east of the line had been cut back considerably. At the opposite end of the platform was the new signalbox, whilst in the large yard, west of the line, there was a substantial goods shed. A small shelter was also provided mid way along the platform for passengers awaiting trains. St Agnes was one of the three passing places on the branch and, obviously, one of the most important stations.

On leaving St Agnes the branch curved sharply eastward following a cutting through farmland for no more than a quarter of a mile to Goonbell Halt. Like Mount Hawke it was a single platform in a cutting. It too had a pagoda, and kept it long after the line closed! Beyond Goonbell the line crossed the impressive viaduct of the same name. This masonry structure of five arches

A view of Goonbell viaduct under construction in 1902. The photograph shows clearly the manner in which the structure was built, with the arches resting on a sturdy timber framework giving the masonry the important initial support. Note the crane set on its own bridging and running rails. *Royal Institution of Cornwall*

bears the inscription, 'J.C. Inglis 1903', the company's chief engineer until his appointment that same year as General Manager. Having crossed Goonbell viaduct the line soon curved northward again passing Mithian Halt heading for Perranporth and the sea on a falling gradient.

At Perranporth the simple concrete platform and shelter comprising the Beach Halt, opened in July 1931. It stood in sharp contrast to the main station itself a quarter of a mile beyond. At eight miles from Chacewater, Perranporth was a stylish and spacious structure built in anticipation of handling important tourist traffic. It was built on the island platform principle and was a passing place. A signalbox, goods shed and cattle pens added to its standing in railway terms, but more than anything the station was the gateway to the magnificent golden beach nearby; to the extensive sand dunes, sea air and cliff scenery. The former mining village developed as a holiday and residential centre, a convalescent home also being established there in 1911 and a golf course opening in 1928. Its growing reputation was acknowledged by the provision of the beach halt and by the fact that much later, in the 1950s, a through train on summer Saturdays worked to and from Paddington.

Leaving Perranporth the line turned southward, inland once more along the Bolingey Valley. Climbing out of the valley the line crossed the attractive Goonhavern viaduct with the engine house of an abandoned mine alongside to the west. The railway bisected Goonhavern village itself crossing beneath what is now

Left: Goonbell Halt on the Chacewater – Newquay branch. This typical wayside halt opened like all the other halts on the branch on 16th August 1905. It comprised a simple brick-built platform with a corrugated 'pagoda' style waiting room and two oil lamps. The halt was sited in a cutting on the falling gradient between St. Agnes and Goonbell viaduct, further eastward.
Redruth Local Studies Library

Below: Perranporth station in the early years of the line. Note the 'almost new' condition of the goods shed and station roofing and the general state of order prevailing. Perranporth had an island platform built to very generous dimensions. Trains leaving for St Agnes and Truro followed a very sharp curve to the left on leaving the station running behind the main part of the town itself. Notice the close proximity to the sand dunes and sea underlining Perranporth's image as a tourist resort.
Royal Institute of Cornwall

The 1.35 pm Newquay – Truro leaving Perranporth behind '4575' class tank No. 5552. 20th May 1959. Trains running from Perranporth to St Agnes faced a long, fierce climb; maximum load for '4500'/'4575' class locomotives on the branch was 170 tons. *M. Mensing*

Perranporth, as seen from a train arriving from St Agnes. Passenger access to the station was via a subway beyond the water column and corrugated hut. Being an island platform, access was difficult for any parcels or the like needing to be loaded or unloaded from the platforms. The train is the 1.35 pm Chacewater – Newquay. 20th May 1959. *M. Mensing*

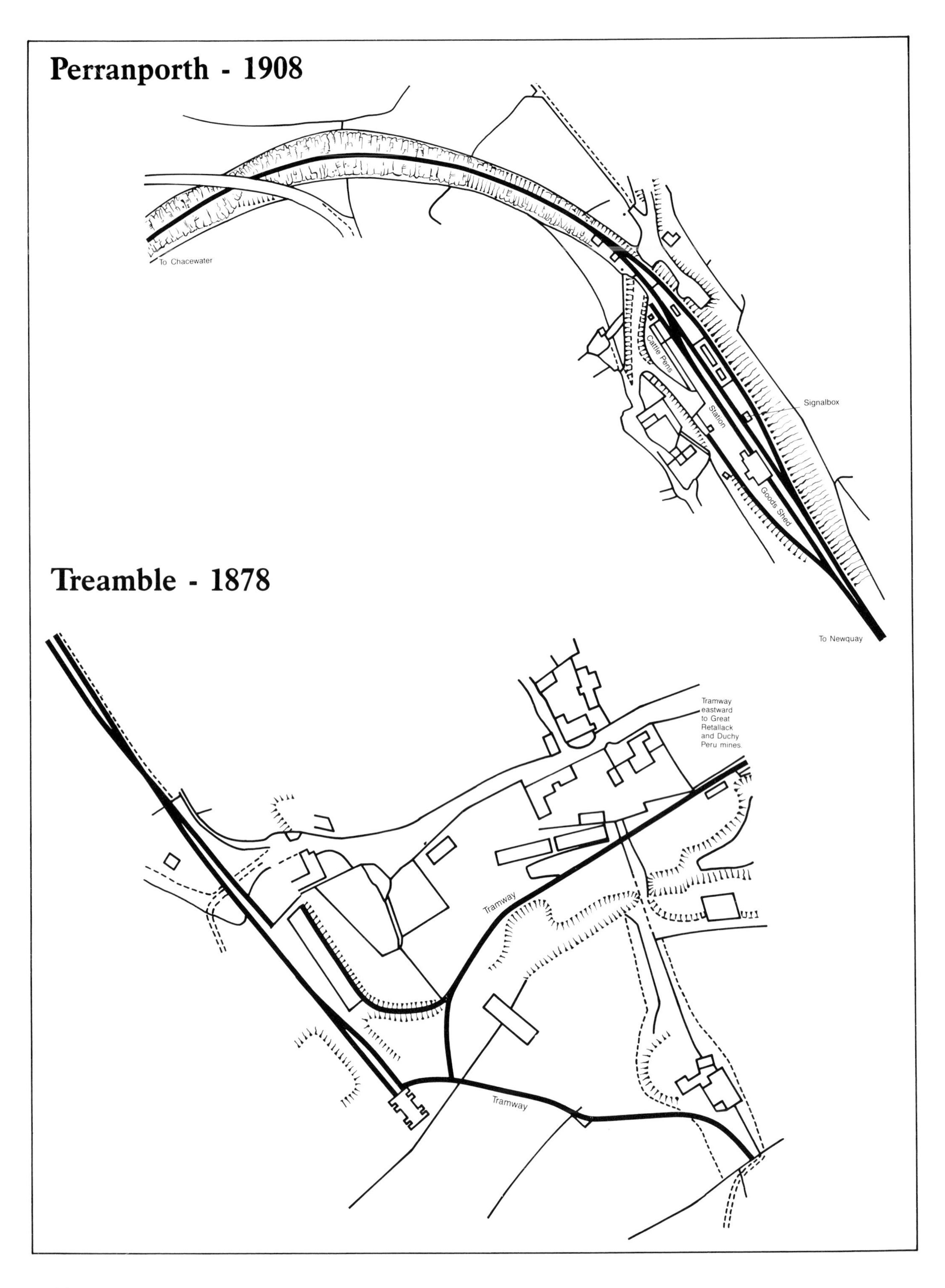
Perranporth - 1908
To Chacewater
Cattle Pens
Station
Signalbox
Goods Shed
To Newquay
Treamble - 1878
Tramway eastward to Great Retallack and Duchy Peru mines.
Tramway
Tramway

A busy period at Perranporth on 3rd August 1959. The 4.39 pm Chacewater – Newquay is seen at the platform, doubleheaded by '4575' class Nos. 5546 and 5539. No. 5515 is approaching the station with the 4.35 pm Newquay – Chacewater. Nothing remains today of this station, but Perranporth continues to grow as a popular holiday resort. *P. Gray*

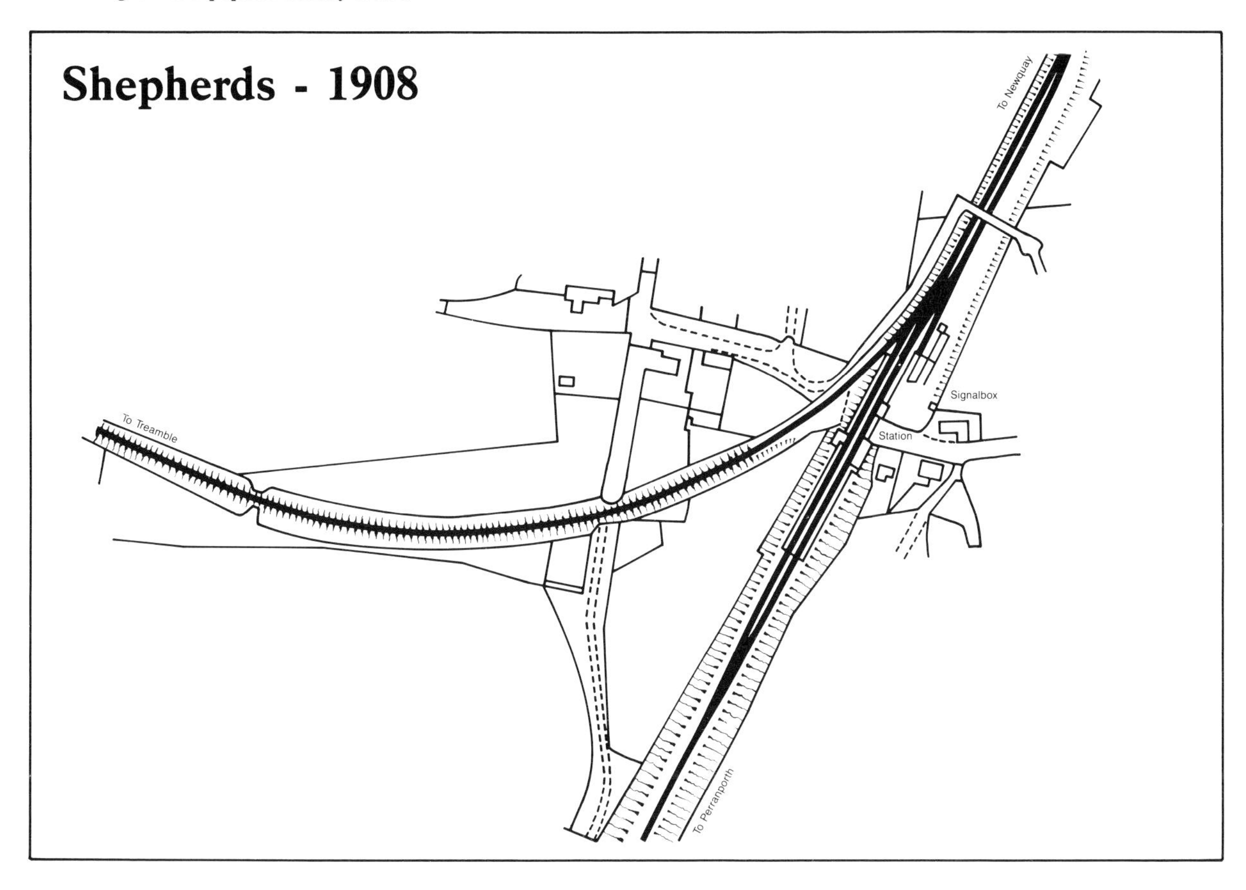

the A3075 Newquay – Redruth road. Goonhavern was another of the simple style halts for the small community there. It comprised a single platform with a pagoda and two oil lamps, and was located to the east of the village being unusually well sited for its passengers.

The line then continued on an east/north-east course towards Shepherds and the junction with the mineral line running westward into the Perran Iron district. Shepherds, 12½ miles from Chacewater, was another passing place and one of the three original stations of January 1905. The main buildings and signalbox were on the east side of the line together with some short sidings. A small waiting room was also provided on the opposite platform. Entering from the Newquay direction, the Treamble line curved away westward. Mineral traffic over this line for Newquay and Fowey has been considered in earlier pages, but it needs only to conclude that beyond Shepherds, the line was lifted (1917) and replaced again for reworking in February 1926. The line closed finally on 1st January 1952 having been disused since the summer of 1949.

From Shepherds to Tolcarne Junction there are interesting contrasts in landscape. Curving first eastward and then to the north, the line passed Mitchell and Newlyn Halt on an embankment above the remains of East Wheal Rose Mine. The latter had its own siding in the early days of mineral working, like many of the mines served by the line. At East Wheal Rose, the siding ran southward on the east side of the branch adjacent to the hamlet of Nanhellan. Mitchell and Newlyn Halt, 1¼ miles beyond Shepherds, was a particularly isolated location, the original wooden platform being later replaced by a concrete structure with a corrugated shelter. For the interested traveller, the railway embankment gave an excellent view of the former rich and extensive lead mining sett as the line turned northward through the Lappa Valley. Passing Benny Mill, the line followed more wooded surroundings close to the Elizabethan Trerice House. Trewerry and Trerice Halt was the last stop before Newquay, three mile distant. It was another simple halt which, like Mitchell and Newlyn, had been rebuilt with a concrete platform. Continuing northwest the branch passed Trevemper siding west of the line to reach Tolcarne Junction, a passing place and the link with the Par – Newquay route. Trevemper siding was the only section of the line to survive the branch closure in February 1963. Chacewater – Newquay trains used the island platform at the terminus where, for obvious reasons, they were overshadowed by services to and from Par.

Passenger services on the line were light but steady during winter and frequently heavy during summer. Freight traffic could not compare with the route via Par, but a steady traffic prevailed. A 40 mph speed limit applied, journey times being approximately one hour. With ten intermediate stops timings varied little, the extremely short distances between stops, heavily graded sections and the circuitous route put obvious limitations on the line. A weekday pattern of nine through trains in each direction and four on Sundays was the arrangement in the early 1930s and traffic held up well until closure. Like the majority of the Cornish branches Churchward 4500 and 4575 2-6-2T locomotives served the line in its later years. These were shedded at Truro, 83F, and were ideal for traffic requirements on the branch. Class 22 diesel hydraulics and DMU sets handled services with the run-down and closure of Truro to steam by 1962.

A personal recollection of the line in its final years, indicative of its summer traffic, was that of a hopelessly overcrowded three coach corridor train to Newquay. The train was so heavily loaded from Chacewater that two passengers fainted from the overcrowding and heat; at St Agnes the train was held whilst the unfortunate travellers were revived with fresh air and water. The incident took place at Whitsun 1958: five years later the line had closed. The last day of service was 4th February 1963 and many local people turned out along the route to witness the last train. Thus, the line had a full working life of only 58 years. As a duplicate route in a rural area, faced with growing competi-

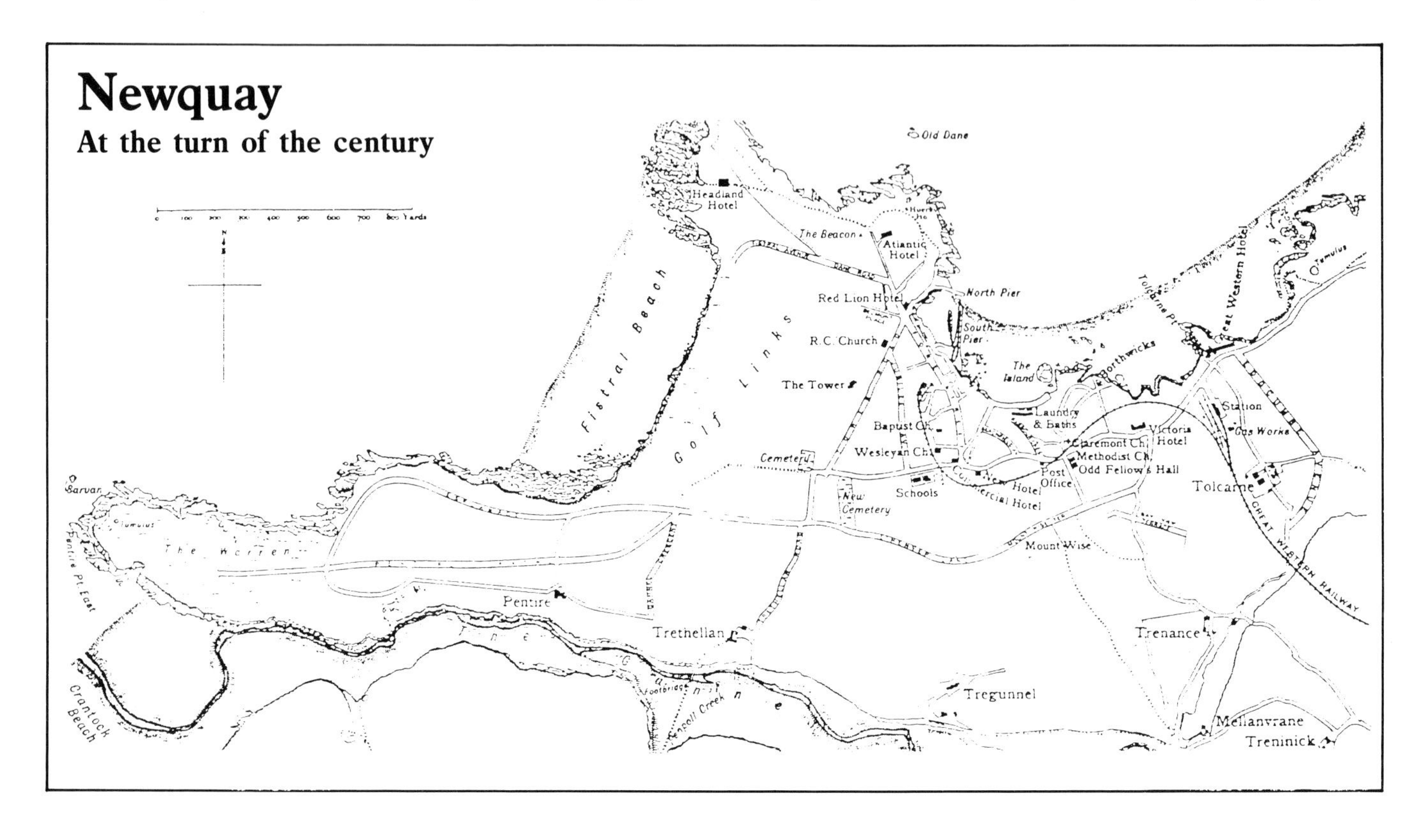

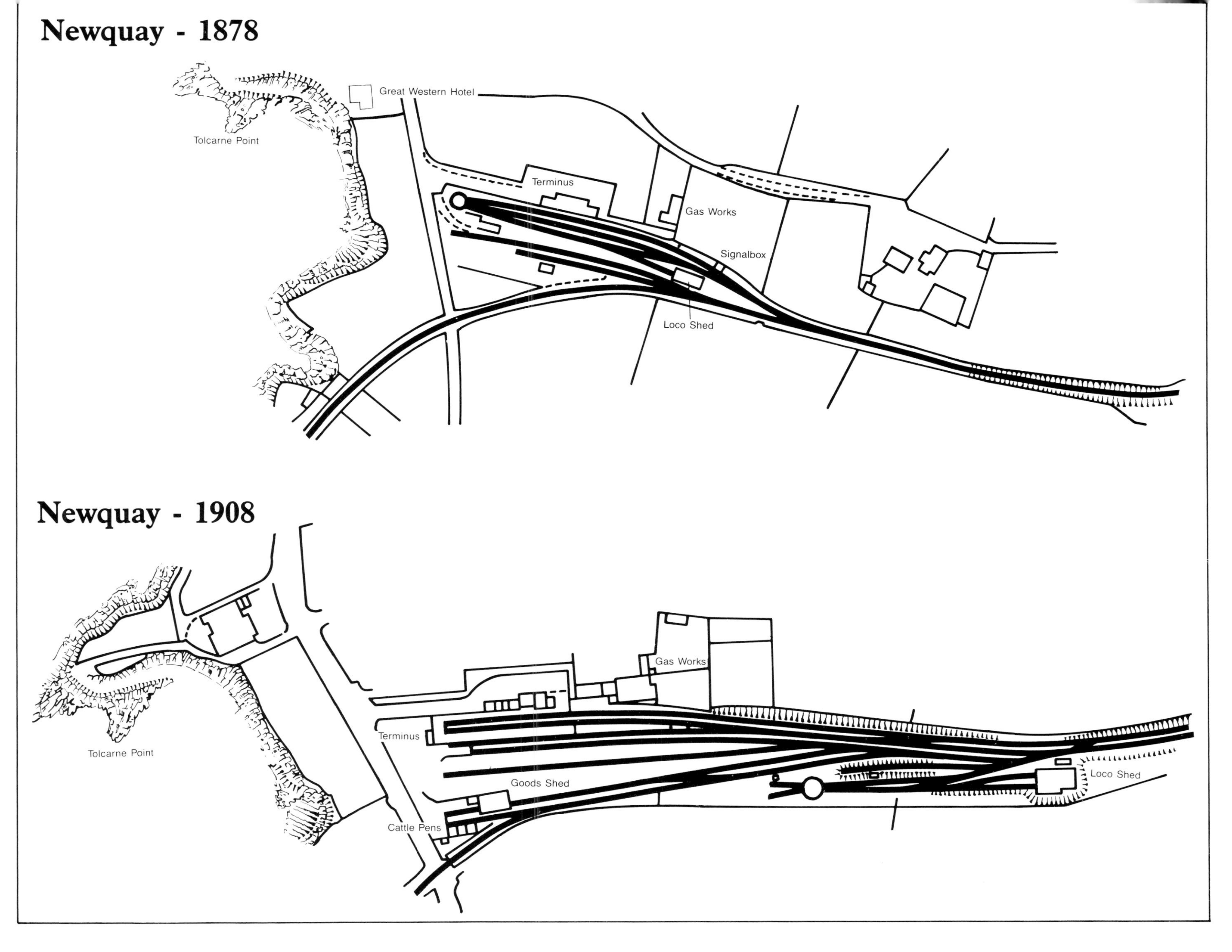

Newquay - 1878
Great Western Hotel
Tolcarne Point
Terminus
Gas Works
Signalbox
Loco Shed
Newquay - 1908
Gas Works
Terminus
Tolcarne Point
Goods Shed
Loco Shed
Cattle Pens

'4575' class No. 5519 stands at platform one at Newquay waiting with the 3.20 pm to Chacewater on 20th May 1959. Corridor coaches were common on this branch, as they made it reasonably easy to board or leave the train from the numerous small halts en route. Platform one was normally the accommodation for Par – Newquay services. *M. Mensing*

tion by road, and the economics of the Beeching Plan, the branch was doomed.

Relatively little remains of the branch today. The triangular junction at Blackwater is still to be seen but at the other end of the line, Tolcarne Junction has vanished under a housing development. Of the stations, St Agnes has been well renovated and Mitchell and Newlyn Halt survives amongst the bushes and trees. Mount Hawke, Goonbell, Mithian and Goonhavern for example, have now disappeared almost entirely without trace except in some cases, for a reasonably defined overbridge. Perranporth and Shepherds are lost to the world and all along the route the trackbed is heavily overgrown; bridges are blown, but the viaducts survive at Goonbell and Goonhavern. The narrow gauge Lappa Valley Railway now operates, however, over a short section of the line from Benny Mill southward to the great mining sett at East Wheal Rose near the village of Newlyn East.

Like the Helston branch further west, the Chacewater – Newquay route was a modest railway that served a rather isolated community quietly and well. Possibly its claim to fame was the through summer Saturday service from Perranporth to Paddington, popular in the late 1950s. As a double-headed working with corridor coaches and restaurant car it made an extremely interesting and impressive sight pounding its way through the quiet rural halts. Like everything connected with the branch, it belongs now to the past, and today's visitors to Newquay, Perranporth or St Agnes could easily be unaware that the line had ever existed.

Chapter Six

China Clay - Origins

The 20¾ mile branch from Par to Newquay was once part of an extensive rail network built during the course of the last century to exploit the vast mineral wealth of the area. Railway development was originally the work of the leading local industrialist J.T. Treffry, of Fowey, known for his interests in Fowey Consols mine, Par harbour and the Cornwall Railway.

During the 1840s Treffry opened three lines to provide outlets at Par and Newquay for the increasing traffic in granite, clay and minerals from his estates. From the early 1840s a line was gradually opened from Ponts Mill to Molinnis, near Bugle. It involved the construction of the Carmears Incline, 947 yards long at a gradient of 1 in 10, and the Treffry viaduct/aqueduct, 216 yards long and 98 feet high crossing the Luxulyan Valley. The incline was worked by water wheels at the summit drawing wagons by wire ropes, the water being provided by means of a specially constructed course, crossing the viaduct itself in a separate channel set below the railway. A branch also led away from the east end of the viaduct to the granite quarries at Colcerrow and was opened c1841. The traffic was horse-drawn, in wagons running on light 'T' rails set into square granite sleeper blocks. In 1855 the line was extended southward from Ponts Mill to Par harbour, replacing a canal worked from 1842. The line to Rock Quarry, or Freeman's Quarry from Ponts Mill was also in operation at this time.

By late 1849 two further lines were completed. In November a railway linked Newquay harbour with Hendra, giving access to the important clay producing district inland near St Dennis (later extended via an incline to Hendra Downs 1857 and worked by stationary engine). A branch from Treloggan, (later, Tolcarne Junction) 1½ miles beyond Newquay, also linked the East Wheal Rose Mine, some five miles to the south west near the village of Newlyn East. This line opened in February 1849, but by this time East Wheal Rose was clearly past its best. The first consignment of lead ore to be carried by rail to Newquay harbour amounted to 30 tons, this being on 26th February 1849. Production at East Wheal Rose had reached its peak in 1845 when output was recorded at 6,885 tons. Within a decade it had decreased to 2,342 tons with closure taking place for all deep mining

An extremely attractive composition reflecting the beauty of the Luxulyan Valley and the grandeur of Treffry's aqueduct/viaduct crossing the valley. '4575' class 2-6-2T No. 5551 heads a heavy branch working, the 2.40 pm Par to Newquay, up the heavy gradient, 1 in 37 at its worst. '5700' class 0-6-0T No. 8702 is at the rear of the train acting as banker. The Treffry aqueduct/viaduct, completed in 1843, carried Treffry's early tramroad from Ponts Mill to Mollinnis across the valley. When the Cornwall Mineral Railway developed the rail system locally, it built a new line, opened in 1874, through the valley to Luxulyan itself. Built of granite, Treffry's magnificent structure was 98 feet high and 216 yards long. 8th August 1959.

P. Gray

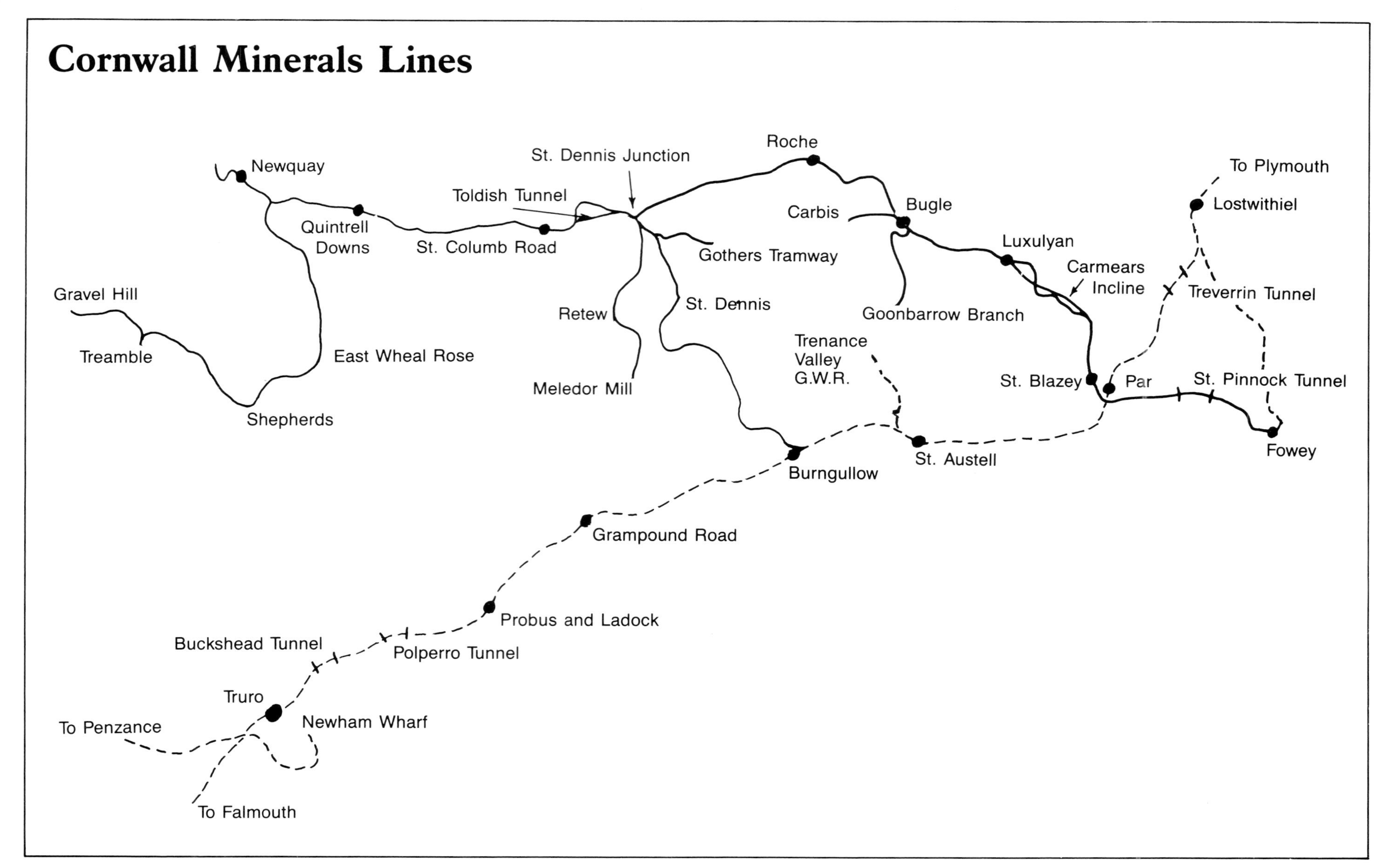

Cornwall Minerals Lines
Newquay
St. Dennis Junction
Roche
To Plymouth
Toldish Tunnel
Lostwithiel
Carbis
Bugle
Quintrell Downs
St. Columb Road
Gothers Tramway
Luxulyan
Carmears Incline
Gravel Hill
Treverrin Tunnel
Retew
St. Dennis
Goonbarrow Branch
Trenance Valley G.W.R.
Treamble
East Wheal Rose
St. Blazey
Par
St. Pinnock Tunnel
Meledor Mill
Shepherds
Fowey
St. Austell
Burngullow
Grampound Road
Probus and Ladock
Buckshead Tunnel
Polperro Tunnel
Truro
Newham Wharf
To Penzance
To Falmouth

Above: An overhead view from the Treffry aqueduct as No. 6858 *Woolston Grange*, and Churchward 2-6-0 No. 6397, climb the valley on the 10.45 am Par – Newquay on 19th July 1958. Gradients as steep as 1 in 37 and 1 in 40 made this sustained climb something of an ordeal for heavily loaded, westbound holiday trains. The fierce gradients, characterising the line, were the legacy of the line's earliest years as a mineral railway. With assistance, the maximum load for a 'Castle' was 320 tons; 'Granges' and 'Halls', 280 tons; 'Manors' 250 tons. *P. Gray*

Right: Luxulyan, looking southwards, soon after rebuilding in 1910/1911. The island platform was part of a new layout at this station, (known as 'Bridges' until May 1905). Under the original provision, there were two separate platforms with a signalbox at the south (Par) end of the station to the east of the line. The new proposals showed a signalbox immediately east of the island platform, as seen in the photograph. It was fitted with 24 levers. The windmill pumped water for the tank, and new water columns were also provided at both ends of the station.

Redruth Local Studies Library

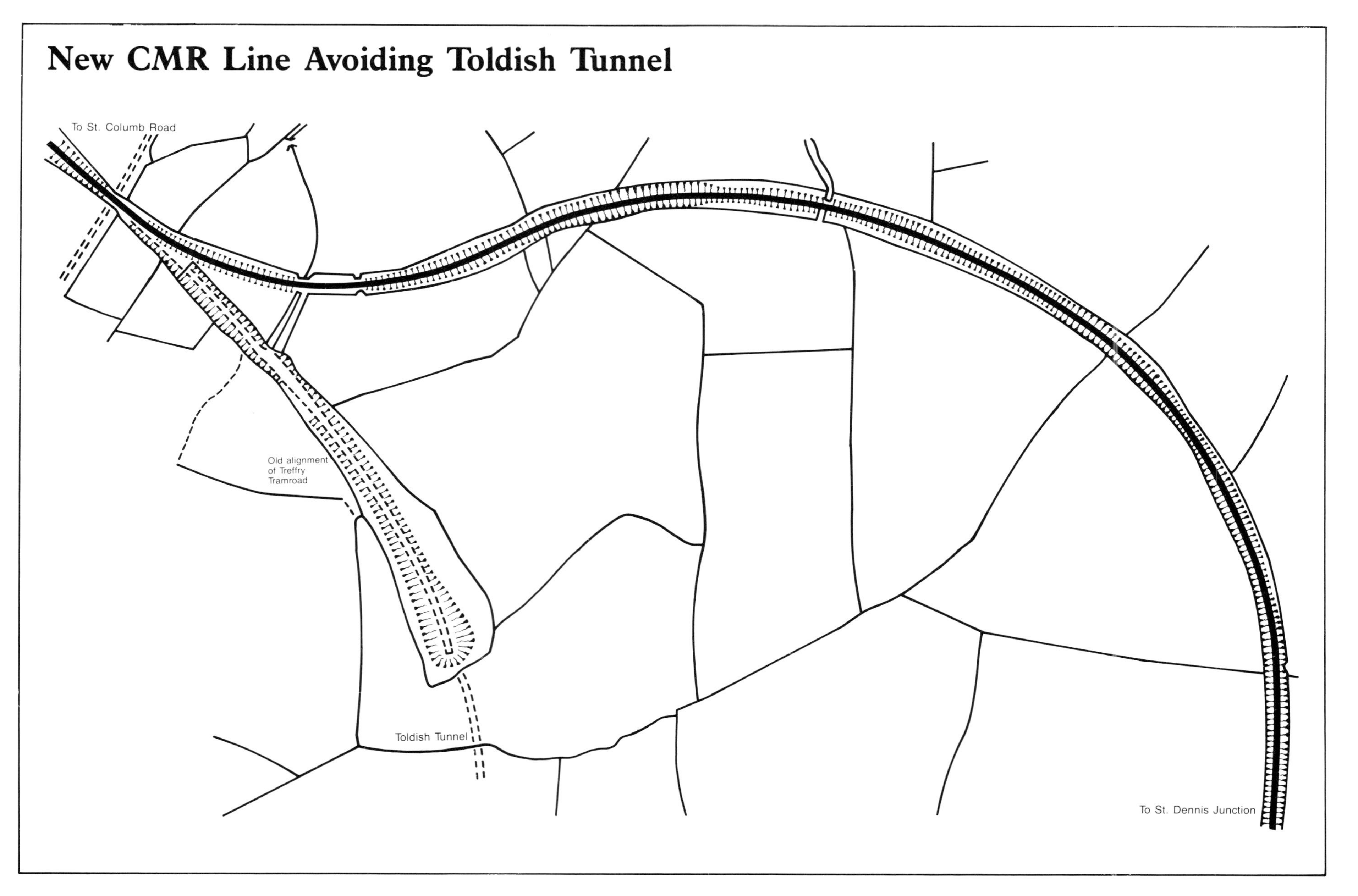
New CMR Line Avoiding Toldish Tunnel
To St. Columb Road
Old alignment
of Treffry
Tramroad
Toldish Tunnel
To St. Dennis Junction

A view in the opposite direction many years later in July 1958. Double-headed 'Halls', Nos. 6931 *Aldborough Hall* and 6941 *Fillongley Hall*, leave Luxulyan on a fine summer's day with the 11.15 am Newquay – Wolverhampton. The station has maintained a high standard of appearance and the water tower has gained in height, and received modifications to the tank itself. The windmill has disappeared. Note the Camping Coach in the sidings, and the booking office with timetables and notices posted outside the main entrance. Leaving the station, the train will begin the steep descent through the Luxulyan Valley to St Blazey and Par. In response to the heavier summer traffic of the present century the crossing loop was extended in 1910 and again, quite substantially in 1936. This was also the case at other stations along the line. *P. Gray*

The Plymouth Railway Circle tour covering the Cornwall Minerals lines on 28th April 1962 is seen here during the lunch stop at Bugle. '4500' class 2-6-2T No. 4564 and '4575' class No. 5531 are in charge of this working, made up of brake-vans, as it stands on the Carbis branch line. Bugle was rebuilt from its original single platform during 1930/31 when double track was laid through the station eastward to Goonbarrow Junction. From that time, Bugle consisted of an island platform, that is, until late in 1964, when the line serving the platform face seen here, the sidings beyond the station and the signalbox, beyond the train, were all removed. *P. Gray*

'5700' class No. 9655 is seen here having left Roche for Newquay on the 1.35 pm service from Par. The train is at the summit of the route between Par and Newquay on 19th July 1958. With its five intermediate stops this train took one hour five minutes to complete the 20¾ mile journey.
P. Gray

by 1858. A further unsuccessful attempt was made to work the mine in the 1880s.

Access to Newquay harbour, also the property of Treffry, was by an 'S' shaped course along what is now the main street. From a point immediately west of the present station the line continued across the main road, turning left to follow it before again crossing on a curve, only to cross yet again to negotiate the descent of the tunnelled incline at 1 in 4½ to the harbour.

A report of June 1860 by Captain H.W. Tyler, linked with proposals for introducing locomotives between Newquay and St Dennis, provides interesting details on the condition of the line at that time.

> 'The greater part of the line is laid with light rails weighing, it is said, 42 lbs to the linear yard, in light chairs in which they are secured by iron keys. The chairs rest upon stone blocks about 3 feet apart from centre to centre. On portions the permanent way is still less substantial; and it is in want of repair for the better transport of the traffic which now passes over it.
>
> There is a timber viaduct near Newquay which would require to be strengthened if locomotive engines were employed and the tunnels and bridges over the line are low and narrow, less than 12 feet high above the rails, by about 10 feet wide.
>
> Under present circumstances, the railway is not fitted for locomotive engines of any description. Besides the condition of the permanent way, the points and crossings upon it are of an inferior description, and would have to be replaced by better ones.'

Treffry's lines provided the basis for the later and more extensive development that took place under the Cornwall Minerals Railway. The latter, incorporated by an Act of 21st July 1873, was empowered to take over Treffry's existing system and to improve and extend it by building a number of new routes serving the clay district. By way of improvement the company constructed an entirely new section from Pontsmill to Bridges (Luxulyan) through the Luxulyan Valley itself. This new section avoided the Carmears Incline and the Treffry aqueduct/viaduct, but it entailed heavy gradients with sections as severe as 1 in 37. Toldish tunnel, further west between Bodmin Road Junction (St Dennis Junction) and Halloon, (St Columb Road) was also avoided by a deviation following a clearly defined curve to the north. (See plan.) Immediately outside Newquay itself, Treffry's original line crossed the Trenance Valley on a timber viaduct set on stone piers. This was 210 yards long and 98 feet high. By 1874 it had been rebuilt; the timbers were replaced by a wrought iron structure that rested directly on extended masonry piers, butressed for extra strength.

The East Wheal Rose branch was also improved with the replacement of three level crossings by bridges and the provision of an east curve at the junction to form a triangle allowing direct access to and from the east. In addition, the branch was extended to Treamble, and, shortly afterwards, beyond to Gravel Hill Mine in the midst of the iron producing area.

In its early development the Minerals Company was concerned primarily with the large-scale movement of iron ore to its deep water port at Fowey. The iron ore came from the Perran Iron Mines north of Perranporth and was said to be both rich and plentiful. Developed by the Cornish Consolidated Iron Mines

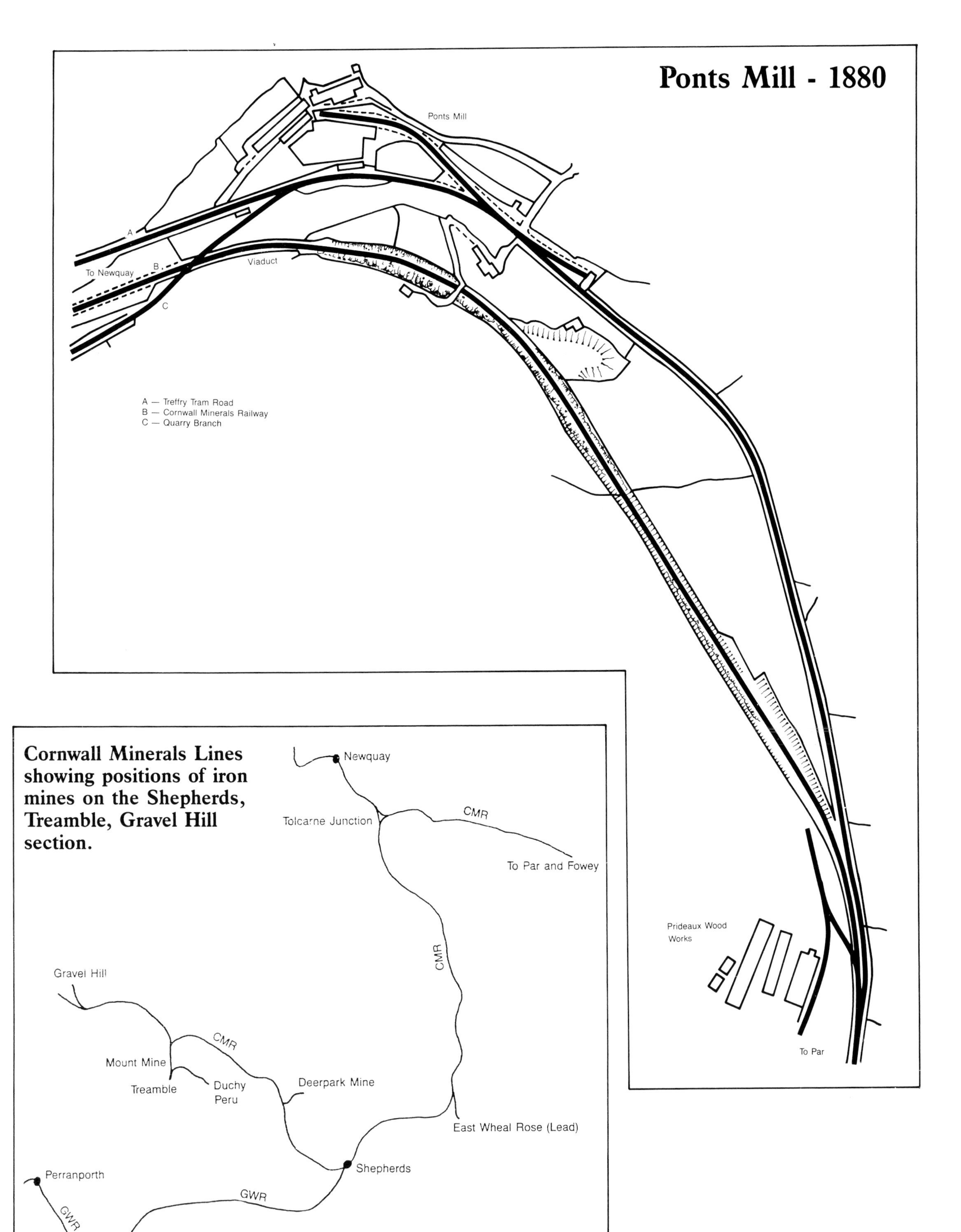
Ponts Mill - 1880
Ponts Mill
A
To Newquay
B
C
Viaduct
A — Treffry Tram Road
B — Cornwall Minerals Railway
C — Quarry Branch
Prideaux Wood
Works
To Par
Cornwall Minerals Lines showing positions of iron mines on the Shepherds, Treamble, Gravel Hill section.
Newquay
Tolcarne Junction
CMR
To Par and Fowey
CMR
Gravel Hill
CMR
Mount Mine
Treamble
Duchy
Peru
Deerpark Mine
East Wheal Rose (Lead)
Shepherds
Perranporth
GWR
GWR

Another double-headed working, this time the 12.30 pm Newquay to Paddington on 19th July 1958. The locomotives, Nos. 6832 and, pilot, 7816, are returning from Newquay with the London train having worked a local service down the branch. This train, of no less than fourteen ex GWR coaches, has crossed Goss Moor and the main A30 road via the bridge to the left of the photograph. The long climb to the summit at Roche is almost complete as the train leaves the open moorland country and enters the cutting leading on towards the summit. *P. Gray*

Corporation, the workings reached south-eastward, inland from the north end of Perran beach. The principal mines were: Gravel Hill, Mount Mine, Treamble, Great Retallack, Duchy Peru and Deerpark.

The CCIMC was incorporated under an Act of 6th April 1872 with capital of £600,000. William Richardson Roebuck was the central figure and apparent prime mover in the formation of the Iron Mines Corporation and the Cornwall Minerals Railway serving it. He was said to have been an assistant to Captain Huish of the LNWR between 1850 and 1860 and was also responsible for bringing the valuable red haematite iron ores from Ulverston and Whitehaven to the South Staffordshire iron district by railway. In all official business relating to the mines, railway and blast furnace interests locally, Roebuck's address was given as 'Trevarthian' St Austell. The local press considered that the CMR was 'largely indebted to Mr Roebuck for the conception of the scheme and the foresight which enabled him to see the immense resources of a yet undeveloped district'.

It was Roebuck's idea to arrange a special tour of the line on 6th June 1874; The host showing 'considerable tact and unceasing courtesy', so it was said, conducted the trip for 'landowners, bankers, lawyers and merchants, whose eyes cannot have failed to have been opened by this process of ocular demonstration'. The party left Par at 8.30 am for Fowey, hauled by the locomotive *Treffry* which was suitably decorated with evergreens, flags and garlands. Accommodation consisted of six mineral trucks which had been suitably prepared for the visit. Having toured the docks at Fowey, where over 700 tons of iron ore was awaiting shipment, the party then returned, proceeding to Newquay. From there, the train took them to Treamble, 'and thence over an extension line of a mile and a quarter into the midst of the Perran sand hills, and within a short walk of the cliff known as Gravel Hill, to the eastern extremity of Perran Beach'. According to the visitors that day the coast was 'literally iron bound'. The account of the activities seen at this location continued:

> 'Strong gangs of men are burrowing into the face of the rock and have already raised an immense pile of brown haemetite on the beach. Here, as at Treamble, operations are carried on by open quarrying, but a shaft is also being sunk from the surface, and an engine house is in process of erection for an engine to be used in pumping and in drawing up the ore from the beach on an inclined plane of very steep gradient, whence the trucks will run another short distance down another tramway and be tipped into trucks attached to the locomotive engine. We made our way back to Treamble, where the operation of dynamite blasting was witnessed, in the immense quarry which has been cleared of iron ore, and we duly marvelled over the 60 or 70 thousand tons of brown haemetite ready for transferring to the railway trucks. Here, calcining works are in the course of erection, for the purpose of reducing the bulk of the ore before carriage.'

It was also pointed out to the visitors that the extension line from Treamble to Gravel Hill, over a distance of one mile and four chains, had been completed in ten days. Parliamentary permission had not been obtained for this line. In conclusion, the party was told of the intention 'to convert Par into another Middlesbrough', and with a tremendous sense of optimism enjoyed by all, the party returned to Par. As part of the overall development blast furnaces were also planned for Par and Fowey.

Above: No. 4976 *Warfield Hall* pilots North British class '22' diesels D6321 and D6310 on the 10.00 am Newquay–Paddington on 9th July 1960. The train, comprising fifteen coaches, is negotiating the curve east of St Columb Road which was laid by the Cornwall Minerals Railway to avoid the original Treffry line through Toldish tunnel. *P. Gray*

Right: Newquay before World War One. A train for Par stands at platform one. The island platform was added here as part of the improvements and extensions of 1905, providing for the newly opened line from Chacewater/Perranporth. The station was much enlarged on several occasions during the later years of the GWR with the 'up' platform being extended in 1928 and 1934 and the island platform in 1938. *Royal Institution of Cornwall*

Despite the optimism, with the confident predictions that the mines could produce five to six thousand tons per day, there was a markedly less hopeful outlook at the Fourth Ordinary Meeting of the CMR in February 1875. With reference to the mines and their traffic it was stated:

> 'Owing partly to the stagnation of the iron trade, but chiefly to the Corporation not having completed their arrangements for working the mines more efficiently, the guaranteed traffic has hitherto almost totally failed.'

Figures for the two years 1873 and 1878 for the county overall reflect the decisive slump in production between these dates. A total output of 31,455 tons to the value of £25,334 10s 2d was given for 1873, the iron ore being produced from 23 mining setts from which returns were available. By 1878 output was only 1,308 tons at a value of £879 16s; production being based on only three mines. The Iron Mines Corporation was finally dissolved in April 1884. Four years later, the rail extension from Treamble to Gravel Hill was also abandoned.

Journey's end: No. 1419 stands at the Par end of Fowey station. The line ahead was the original Cornwall Minerals route to Par and Newquay opened in 1874. Pinnock tunnel, 1173 yards long and the longest in the county, was an important engineering feature between Par and Fowey, as indeed, were the heavy gradients in both directions entailing 1 in 40 and 1 in 50. Passenger services between Fowey and Par ceased in July 1929 and freight in 1968 when the route was converted to a roadway for lorries carrying clay to the port. *P.Q. Treloar*

The newly constructed 4-mile extension from Par to Fowey was a most significant development. It gave direct access to the deep-water port at Fowey and was the final link in the 24½ mile route from Newquay across the county. Like the rest of the line it involved heavy gradients. From Fowey the line climbed a fierce 1 in 36 to Pinnock tunnel, 1,173 yards long, and then fell at 1 in 50 to Par. Pinnock tunnel was the longest in Cornwall and was constructed by working from both ends and from five shafts along its course. By contrast, Coswarth tunnel, between St Columb and Quintrell Downs, was only 44 yards long; Luxulyan tunnel was longer at 50 yards.

Together with the route from Fowey to Newquay, the 1873 Act specified the construction of the following lines into the clay district. Bugle to Carbus, one mile 50 chains; (later known as Carbis) St Dennis Junction to Melangoose Mill, 2 miles 5 chains; (known as the Retew branch) and Hendra to Drinnick Mill. The latter was intended to make a junction with the broad gauge Newquay and Cornwall Junction Railway running westward from Burngullow on the Cornwall Railway. The N&CJR (authorised on 14th July 1864) opened initially as far as Drinnick Mill on 1st July 1869, but was unable to complete to St Dennis because of financial difficulties.

Above: '4200' class 2-8-0 No. 4206 pounds up the bank from Fowey with china clay empties for Par on 15th June 1956. This section is now a roadway for china clay traffic carried by lorry the railway being closed in 1968. *M. Mensing*

Right: Another view of No. 4206 on clay empties, this time with a train which has just passed beneath the viaduct carrying the Cornish main line. Par Bridge signalbox controlled movement to and from the harbour and at the south end of St Blazey yard. An overall speed limit of 25 mph applied on the line with a 15 mph restriction being observed on the section here, passing Par Dock, Par Bridge and St Blazey yard. 8th September 1955. *P. Gray*

Above: St Dennis Junction looking southward towards Burngullow. '4500' class No. 4526 runs round a Plymouth Railway Circle 'special' visiting the clay branches, whilst '5700' class No. 3705 arrives with a freight off the Retew branch. 1st October 1955. *P. Gray*

Left: No. 4526 at Drinnick Mill with its PRC 'Special' comprising six GWR 'toad' brake-vans. The locomotive is taking water whilst a small group of railwaymen pose unofficially for the camera on 1st October 1955. Unlike many locations on the former GWR clay lines, Drinnick Mill continues to provide substantial clay traffic today. *P. Gray*

This line served the important clay producing district within the parishes of St Mewan, St Stephens-in-Branwell and St Dennis. With an estimated capital of £27,000, which soon proved inadequate, the line was completed only after considerable difficulty and delay. The works were heavy, requiring expensive cuttings through granite together with severe curvatures and steep gradients of up to 1 in 40, 1 in 50 and even a section at 1 in 34. No tunnels or viaducts were needed. Finances were not always available with the result that work was erratic. Breaks in construction meant that five years separated the Act of Incorporation from the actual opening to Drinnick and the West of England Clay Company. On completion, the contractor, William West and Son of St Blazey, was owed a considerable sum of money; he also worked the line in its earliest years until its transfer to the CMR.

Despite obvious problems, the opening day was something of an occasion. A special train of four coaches headed by the locomotive *Newquay* left St Austell for Drinnick Mill on Thursday 1st July. As with all such events the locomotive was 'gaily decorated with flowers and flags, the train conveying officials and their friends over the new route, leaving St Austell at 1pm'. A band from Fowey accompanied them, the journey from the junction at Burngullow taking some sixteen minutes. At Drinnick the party was provided with luncheon at the works itself followed by the return trip leaving at 3pm. A celebratory dinner was also held in St Austell to mark the occasion with many guests that evening representing railway and clay manufacturing interests. Amongst the speakers, William West drew applause for his work on the line and for his observation that Drinnick and the clay works along the route would provide valuable feeder traffic for the Cornwall Railway. He also stated that 'there was no question that the line would eventually reach Newquay'. This was much appreciated, but circumstances did not allow any further work beyond Drinnick until 1873 when the CMR took charge.

The minerals company built their part of the overall link from Hendra (St Dennis) to Drinnick to the standard gauge, whereas the original Act stated that the line should be of mixed gauge to give access to broad gauge traffic. Following a legal dispute the broad gauge was eventually installed, but only to comply with the letter of the law. Broad gauge trains did not, in fact, use the Drinnick Mill – St Dennis section because of the poor quality of the track. Drinnick Mill became, in effect, yet another instance of a break of gauge within the county.

Four months before the official opening of the CMR the Engineers Report was presented to the second General Meeting of the company in London in February 1874. The engineer was Mr W.H. Thomas, and the contractor, Sir Morton Peto. W.H. Thomas' report read as follows:

'The progress made during the past six months at all parts of the line has been very satisfactory, and in a few weeks the railway from Fowey to Treamble will be in a sufficiently finished state for opening for mineral traffic. The wharves and jetties at Fowey are in a forward state. Between Fowey and the tunnel the earthworks are practically complete and permanent way and ballasting are commenced.

In the tunnel itself there remains but 100 lineal yards to complete. This represents a short month's work, and at the western end the permanent road is being laid. The line is finished all but permanent way from the tunnel to Polmear, at which point the road is crossed by a bridge; this only requires the girders. Works are finished, the road laid across Par Sands, and the crossing of the canal and river at Par is effected.

At the depot work has not gone on so well as I could have wished, the delay having been chiefly caused by the difficulty in obtaining other materials, and it will be a hard matter to get the running shed and tank-house finished by the time the line is ready for opening.

From Par to St Blazey the permanent way is laid and ballasted. On railway No. 2 the heaviest works on the whole system and those which will take the longest time to complete occur. The two granite cuttings above Ponts Mill are being pushed to the utmost, and from an inspection made this week I think they can be cleared out in five or six weeks from this date. Immediately above the last named work in a large viaduct, the manner of which will not be out of hand for a fortnight and after that the girders will take some weeks to rivet up. At the northern end of the viaduct there is a considerable gap in the embankment, which, at the highest point, is 40 feet deep. I am of the opinion that this can be filled up in about six weeks. Passing up the Luxulyan Valley, the works, with the exception of some embanking which is being made from side cutting, made be said to be finished as far as Rock Mill. Here there is a long cutting in hard granite which will take three or four weeks to finish. The large cutting at Luxulyan village will require about the same time to get out. From Luxulyan to Bugle the tramway has been reconstructed, the permanent way laid and ballasted. There are two public road bridges with heavy approaches on this portion of the line, which are rather backward but I believe that they will be finished about the same time as the remainder of the works.

Railway No. 3 is in a forward state with the exception of the long embankment crossing the road at Goss Moor which still wants 13,000 cubic yards to complete it, a great portion of this coming from side cutting. I do not anticipate that a longer time will be requisite to finish this section than will be necessary for railway No. 2.

The only works of importance outstanding on railway No. 4 are the cuttings at Fiddlers' Green and Rejourra, and the stone fencing generally on the line. The latter requires a strong force to ensure its being completed in time for the opening.

On the tramway between Newquay and St Dennis the permanent way is now laid for a length of five miles. All the bridges on this portion of the work are finished, with the exception of those at White Cross, Halloon and Goss Moor which await the girders.

The tramway from East Wheal Rose to Newquay is finished with the exception of the bridge over at Beny Mill and Matha, both of which are in hand.

The work on the Retew branch is not progressing well, possession having been obtained of all the requisite land, but on the Carbis branch, about one mile in length and easy of construction, ground has not yet been broken. The Newquay and Cornwall Junction line is also rapidly approaching completion, though it will not be ready for opening simultaneously with the remainder of the system.

With the exception of Fowey, nothing has been done at any of the passenger stations, but there is ample time to erect them before the line is opened for passenger traffic, the spring and summer season being so much more favourable for building operations than the present. Of the rolling stock contracted for, 11 locomotives and 28 wagons have been delivered.'

The main line from Fowey to Newquay was 24½ miles long and rose 600 feet to summit level near Roche, with 1 in 40 gradients on each side. During the course of construction, *The West Briton* included several reports on the activities of the navvies on the line. In December 1872, for example, a young man named Edwards was killed by an explosion of dynamite, ironically, just as he had finished reading instructions giving warning to keep the explosive away from stoves or fireplaces. Whilst carrying out the instructions, the dynamite exploded. In keeping with custom, there was a large turnout amongst the navvies from this part of the line at the funeral.

Whilst society did not generally express any great anxiety over the suffering frequently experienced by navvies, the latters' apparent disregard, or absence, of religious observances caused considerable attention. Navvies were frequently denounced for their failure to observe the Sabbath. A letter to *The West Briton* signed, *Observer*, St Columb, 9th March 1874, was typical of its kind:

'One of the most glaring acts of Sabbath-breaking which as ever come under my notice was committed on Sunday last. The Cornwall

Minerals Railway Company have for some weeks past been carrying on operations between Halloon and Goss Moor. On Sunday last about 50 or 60 navvies were employed laying the metals and a locomotive was kept constantly running, bringing ballast etc. Horses and carts were also brought into requisition: in fact, the whole day was spent in every respect as an ordinary working day, and with an utter disregard of the Sabbath. Such a desecration of the Lord's-day in this part of the county is not in the remembrance of the oldest inhabitant, and is to be deeply regretted for many reasons. As an inducement to work, the men were promised a plentiful supply of beer, and it is reported that all who refused to labour were threatened with instant dismissal!'

The Cornwall Minerals Railway opened to traffic on 1st June 1874. There was little in the way of ceremony; the event being described as 'a purely business matter, conducted in a purely business way'. A special excursion over the line was provided, however, on Saturday 6th June in connection with the Royal Cornwall Show, held at St Austell, and has already been covered in connection with the business of the Iron Mines Corporation.

A matter of days before the opening there was an accident involving a heavy clay train of 130 tons. It got into difficulty when it lost control on the descent of Luxulyan bank. The weight of the train was too great to hold and it ran off the track in a cutting near Pontsmill. The derailment was the direct result of a broken rail believed to have been caused by a combination of the speed and weight of the train. The fireman, John Rowe, was described as 'seriously wounded', whilst the brakesman, William Opie, suffered an injury to an eye. The driver was reported as 'much shaken'. Staff moved quickly to repair the broken line, clear the debris from the shattered wagons and remove the clay thrown across the cutting. The General Manager, Mr Richardson, was therefore able to start the first official mineral train from Par according to plan.

Motive power for the company was provided through an order for eighteen locomotives from the Atlas Works of the Sharp-Stewart Co., Manchester. These were originally 30 ton 0-6-0 side tanks with 3′6″ wheels, and were progressively rebuilt from 1883. The last of these locomotives was withdrawn in 1936. Four hundred and twenty four-ton trucks were also ordered. These were of iron and wood and were to carry 12 tons laden. The chief offices, workshops and locomotive sheds were at Par. They were brick built on a site that was formerly waste ground. The locomotive sheds consisted of nine bay units constructed in a fan shape, with each line leading out to the turntable. It was a variation on the roundhouse design. Repair sheds, an erecting shop, fitting shops, boiler makers and smiths' shops, together with separate accommodation for a wagon department ensured that the company was well provided to meet its requirements.

A further development made possible by the opening of the CMR was of the construction of the Gothers Tramways linking the clay pits at Gothers with the minerals company a short distance south of St Dennis Junction on the line to Burngullow. The tramway opened following the acquisition of the Gothers clay pits by H.D. Pochin in 1879. These workings were to the north east of St Dennis itself with the tramway (3 foot gauge) running south-eastward for approximately five miles from its link alongside the CMR. Sleeper timbers on this line came from old wooden warships which had been broken up at the naval dockyard at Devonport.

St. Dennis Junction on a fine summer's day in July 1955. 0-6-0 PT '5700' class No. 3635, with a 2-6-2T '4500' class No. 4526 banking, heads away for St. Blazey and Fowey. St. Dennis Junction signalbox and the lines to Burngullow and Meledor Mill can also be seen leading away here.
R.C. Riley

Chapter Seven

China Clay - Development of Traffic

Together with the failure of the expected iron ore traffic, the CMR had also to contend with a depression in the china clay industry through the mid 1870s. Production during 1875 and 1876, so soon after the railway had opened, was the lowest for many years, putting the minerals company in need of support. Output for the years 1873-1877 was as follows:

	Clay	Stone
1873	153,000 tons	45,000 tons
1874	150,000 tons	42,500 tons
1875	108,250 tons	38,000 tons
1876	105,275 tons	34,500 tons
1877	200,345	39,500 tons

The trade depression indicated here resulted in an inevitable decline of traffic; the Cornwall Railway also carrying 41,753 tons less in 1875 than the previous year.

Clay carried by the Cornwall Minerals Railway in 1877 was up by 8,000 tons on 1875.

	Tons
From Bridges Station	417
From Bugle Station	37,943
From Drinnick Mill	92,613
From Halloon Station	191
From Melangoose Mill	11,581
From Par Station	3,384
From Victoria Station	2,739

From 1st October 1877 the Minerals line was worked by the GWR, and on 1st July 1896 the latter took complete control of the company. Three years earlier, however, on 2nd October 1893, the CMR opened its own line from Goodbarrow Junction (Bugle) to Carbean, reflecting valuable progress within the industry through the 1880s. (Production by 1885 was 312,413 tons in total.) This line was 3½ miles long and included the 341 yard Stenalees tunnel. It was built to exploit the clay deposits of the St Austell River valley with such pits as Carbean itself, the Higher and Lower Ninestones works and Goonbarrow. Production was estimated to offer between 30 and 60,000 tons annually. Indeed, within the next twenty years the GWR was projecting a further line into this area, this time from the south. This was to be the Trenance Valley branch to Lansalson, begun in 1913 but delayed by the outbreak of war. The Great Western's gauge conversion in May 1892 was also, of course, a great boost to long distance through traffic in clay, encouraging further development within the industry.

The minerals company was also able in 1893 to take control of the abandoned Lostwithiel and Fowey line. Powers had been obtained for the lease in 1875, but financial pressures forced it to be abandoned in March 1876. Services recommenced on 16th September 1895.

Further development for clay traffic took place from 1910 when, on 26th July, an Act was obtained to extend the Retew branch to Meledor Mill. This extension opened to traffic on 1st July 1912, the line from Melangoose Mill extending 1½ miles. The Meledor Mill line followed the valley of the Fal and had been considered since 1874 as a viable route south-westward to the deep water at St Just Pool on the east bank of the Fal estuary. The CMR had wanted to exploit this in their formative years, and in the immediate post-war period of 1919, when Fowey experienced difficulties handling the extensive trade from post-war boom, independent proposals were considered for a Fal Valley link.

In one instance a clay line was actually taken out of use for a substantial period. From 1909 to 1922 the ex N&CJR from Burngullow to St Dennis Junction was closed on account of the Carpella 'Break'.

The Carpella Mining Company gave notice of its intention to exploit the clay deposits on its land, carrying the railway line. This would inevitably mean closure of this route and, given its importance, the GWR contested the mining company's action. An appeal by the GWR reached the House of Lords, where it was rejected and the railway as a through route was forced to close, albeit temporarily. The line was not restored until 18th April 1922.

By the outbreak of war in 1914 the Cornwall Minerals Railway and the GWR had developed an extensive system of rail links between the clay producing districts manufacturing industry itself, and the ports, primarily Fowey. The latter was by the end of pre-war era, the principal port for exports to all parts of the world, china clay being an invaluable raw material for a whole range of modern industries and a crucial factor in developing both the regional and the international economy. The United States and Germany were the largest markets, their imports in 1912 being valued at £304,948 and £100,298 respectively. Production figures in Cornwall reflected the impressive growth of the industry; four years' figures over a period, 1896-1912, the latter marking the peak of production, are given here.

1896 – 471,809 value: £269,077 including china stone
1901 – 523,427 value: £314,701 including china stone
1909 – 695,967 value: £447,017 including china stone
1912 – 856,239 value: £553,680 including china stone

VARYING FORTUNES 1918-1948

China clay production and traffic levels were badly affected by World War One. The loss of major European markets and the U boat menace in the Atlantic restricted American trade, whilst manpower shortages in the clay pits themselves, and problems with coal supplies resulted in a marked contraction within the industry. The Lostwithiel-Fowey branch was actually closed for part of the war from 2nd April to 1st November 1917 as an economy. A short period of intense production followed the return of peace, as with most other industries in Britain. From a figure slightly in excess of 400,000 tons in 1918 production increased to nearly 800,00 tons in 1920. Thereafter, in 1921, falling dramatically almost to the 1918 level. Again, the fortunes of china clay were largely at one with many other sections of British industry; resulting in the incorporation of English China Clays Ltd. in April 1919 reflecting the post war move towards amalgamation in industry, as in the case of the railways and the cotton industry for example.

Two valuable developments for traffic came soon after the war, in 1920 and 1921. In May 1920 the GWR opened its Trenance Valley branch northward from the main Penzance – Plymouth line just west of St Austell. It opened initially on 1st May 1920 to Bojea sidings but was extended to Lansalson by the 24th of that month. As with the earlier Goonbarrow branch and the Meledor Mill line, clay dries were constructed along the route and traffic returns were positive.

Fowey harbour, however, found it difficult to cope with the scale of trade immediately after the war. Only No. 4 jetty was equipped on modern lines and it was therefore worked to capacity. A new jetty, No. 8, was opened by the GWR on 27th September

The Plymouth Railway Circle tour of April 1962 is seen here propelling the brake van train up the Lansalson branch, with Nos. 4564 and 5531 pushing hard. As can be easily seen here, the branch served an important clay producing district, the line opening throughout on 24th May 1920. The photograph depicts typical scenery from the widespread landscape of the china clay industry in Mid Cornwall. *P. Gray*

A view northward over part of the yard at Carne Point. The accommodation here was extended considerably in the early 1920s, as seen here, the through line being doubled for almost two miles into Fowey itself. Number 8 jetty, opened by the GWR in September 1923, demanded increased sidings for up to 200 wagons. This jetty was a great improvement on the others at the waterside with its emphasis upon mechanisation. The embankment was widened into the river area itself by blasting away sections of the inner cliff face. *English China Clays*

Above: As the photographic caption says: GWR official opening of No. 8 jetty with *SS Edern* loading clay 27th September 1923. The moveable shutes fed by elevators enabled the loading process to be carried out far more swiftly. *English China Clays*

Right: End tipping wagons feeding clay for the conveyor system at No. 8 jetty in the inter war years. The wagons are privately owned by Toyne Carter and Co. of Fowey. Compared with the slower process of loading casks or using gravity shutes, this system enabled Fowey to increase its capacity considerably. This, of course, was crucial in the boom years following the end of World War One, and before the onset of world wide economic depression. *English China Clays*

1923. This new addition provided for ships with a capacity of over 9,000 tons: it was 50 feet wide and gave berthage of 500 feet.

Constructed from steel girderwork supported on twenty three steel cylinders set into the rock, the jetty was equipped with electrically operated conveyor belts, cranes and shutes, and was lit by electricity throughout. No. 8 jetty was furthest up river, west of No. 7 (see plan) extending the total distance along the quayside to some 2,400 feet. Extra siding accommodation was also provided as part of the overall improvement. The following year saw the end of the Carpella 'Break' and the restoration of through workings on the Burngullow – St Dennis route.

Production in the inter-war years peaked in 1927 and 1937. The former saw the highest output for the period overall at 869,232 tons for Devon and Cornwall with 75% for export; in 1937 total production was 830,946 tons, 759,704 tons originating from Cornish pits and 64% going for export. Not surprisingly, the lowest level of production after 1921 was in 1932 when the Depression was at its worst. In that year 508,850 tons were produced overall with 466,027 tons from Cornwall. 72% was exported.

Up to and including the year 1940 shipments through Fowey far outweighed any other port; the best years for rail consignments were 1937 and 1939 with 68,796 tons and 70,113 tons carried respectively. With the outbreak of war, however, and particularly after the German conquest of France in May 1940 and their control of the European Channel ports, shipments of materials were forced to pass through west coast ports. Consignments by rail inevitably increased. The following table shows the effects of the war on Fowey and the growth of rail traffic.

	Fowey	Railway
1939	468,278 tons	70,113 tons
1940	217,908 tons	129,051 tons
1941	48,698 tons	134,587 tons
1942	35,244 tons	138,086 tons
1943	57,370 tons	125,477 tons
1944	92,834 tons	131,399 tons
1945	139,084 tons	137,659 tons

From 1941 and 1943 137,592 tons of china clay also passed through the ports of Bristol and Avonmouth as a wartime expedient. Shipments were made throughout the war and into 1946 but on much reduced levels; 213 tons being recorded for 1945, for example. Another significant expedient for wartime purposes was the Board of Trade requirement of 1942 that production be concentrated on just 23 pits. Over 70 others were required to close. The Lostwithiel – Fowey train service was also discontinued for three separate periods from 1940-1944 totalling just over 2½ years.

With the ending of the war in 1945, Britain was dependant on the rapid growth of the export trade. The China clay industry was, therefore, to play an important part in economic recovery and needed to be equipped to do so. The formation of the massive ECLP (English China Clays, Lovering Pochin and Company Ltd) in October 1932 from the largest producers at that time gave the industry valuable resources, unity and direction. ECLP controlled 75 per cent of the china clay industry with large interests in Devon also. Working practices were modernised with widespread use of electricity and research was encouraged to the benefit of the industry overall. Despite the negative impact of the Depression in the early thirties and the inevitable constraints of World War Two, the industry had established the basis for prosperity in the period after 1945.

Technical development and structural change within the china clay industry during the inter-war years brought its rewards after 1945. The extensive uses of china clay as a raw material inevitably boosted output. Demand by manufacturers at home and importantly abroad in the plastics, paints, cosmetics and paper industries, for example, multiplied as greater consumption, research and application extended the markets. Waste material from the clay pits was also utilised widely in the manufacture of concrete blocks, sales being well advertised in the press before World War Two.

The china clay industry was considered essential to the post-war programme of economic recovery generally, both producers and government being anxious to see a return to prosperity. Coal supplies, a precious commodity in the immediate post-war period, were granted by the Board of Trade for the numerous clay dries alongside the lines as Fowey returned to heavy traffic for export.

Great Western involvement was inevitably limited in terms of time. Nationalisation in 1948 saw the end of the GWR name at least, but outwardly there was no great change. The familiar features of Great Western practice remained until the 1960s, when steam locomotives disappeared in 1962 and branches began to fall victim to closure as the clay industry adjusted itself to changing circumstances and requirements. An account of railway involvement with the modern clay industry is another story, however, that would take us far beyond the reference of the GWR and must be told elsewhere.

Whilst the fortunes of the china clay industry have obviously flourished in the post-war period and the commitment to rail transport has been well maintained, the actual railway network serving the industry has contracted. Along with the conversion of the Par – Fowey route to a roadway and the purchase of the docks in 1968, there were several other closures. The Trenance Valley line to Lansalson closed in July 1964 whilst early in the following year the Carbean or Goodbarrow branch ceased operations. 1966 saw the end of through working between Burngullow and St Dennis Junction, and the Retew branch serving Meledor Mill, extended in 1912, passed into history in 1983.

The china clay industry is truly a Cornish giant, but a benevolent one, and the railway, instrumental to its early growth, continues to be closely identified with its progress.

Clay being loaded into wagons of the West of England China Stone and Clay Company of Drinnick. The wagons to the left have been loaded and are covered with waterproof sheeting to prevent damage to the consignment. Note the wagon covers lying in a heap in the foreground.
English China Clays

Chapter Eight

Harbour Development

Although the CMR was responsible for the extensive development of Fowey, it was not first to exploit the port. This was the work of the Lostwithiel and Fowey Railway. This company was incorporated under an Act of 30th June 1862, authorising them to construct a single broad gauge line 4¾ miles long from Lostwithiel to Carne Point, just over half a mile short of Fowey itself. The contractors were Messrs Mead and Lang of Liskeard who worked in conjunction with the company engineer, Mr Jenkin. From the opening, to its premature closure on 31st December 1879, the line was worked by the Cornwall Railway.

There were no official celebrations on the opening day (1st June 1869) the directors, having an eye to their finances, deciding that celebrations could wait until the line was extended to Fowey. Despite the fact that the latter never took place under that company, there was evidence of an occasion locally. The locomotive *Cato* with wagons and a passenger coach left Lostwithiel at 11am carrying certain 'ladies and gentlemen', and arrived at Carne Point nineteen minutes later. They were met by a large number of people from Fowey and two directors of the company; after a short stay, they returned to Lostwithiel with some sixty passengers. A second trip was made during the afternoon. With the opening of the line the Cornwall Railway provided a regular extra train from Plymouth to Lostwithiel departing Plymouth at 8.35am. The locomotive, on arrival, was sent to Carne Point with clay wagons, and on the first day returned with a consignment of 'railway iron' landed at the new quay from the brigantine, *Hannah Orosdale*.

The Lostwithiel and Fowey Railway Co. anticipated heavy traffic on their line, and prior to opening they have made an extremely ambitious application to the Board of Trade concerning Fowey harbour. They sought a provisional order for the following:

1. The Incorporation of the Fowey Harbour Board, comprising thirteen members to include: two by the Corporation of Lostwithiel; six by the railway company; two by the trustees under the will of Mr Treffry; two by qualified owners of property and ratepayers of Fowey, and one by the same from the people of Polruan.
2. A line of quays on the west side of the harbour between Upper Carne Point and Lower Carne Point, above Caffra Mill Pill; a graving dock in the Pill; a line of quays extending southward from the entrance to the dock; a line of quays extending from the south end of the last mentioned quays; any necessary embankments etc connected with the harbour and dredging.
3. The levying of rates.
4. Powers to borrow £60,000.
5. Powers for 'The Fowey Harbour Board' to act as pilotage and a local authority.

Loading casks by crane at one of the older jetties. Note the wagon turntable for access onto the pier and the horse providing the means of movement.
English China Clays

No. 1419, this time running past the sidings at Carne Point. The docks at Fowey were owned by the GWR who developed them considerably in the late nineteenth and early twentieth centuries. '7400' class pannier tank, No. 7446 is seen here shunting the sidings. A 30 mph speed limit applied on the branch with a further reduction to 15 mph from Carne Point to Fowey itself. *P.Q. Treloar*

Not surprisingly there were objections. The Corporation of Lostwithiel claimed that the plans were an attempt to deprive them, without consent, of their chartered rights over Fowey harbour, and that tolls would be excessive and injure trade. The people of Fowey also protested at what threatened to be something of a takeover of the area by the railway company and they pointed to the constitution of the proposed Board with its heavy weighting of railway interests. Moreover, it was said that there was no security for the sum of £60,000 to be borrowed, and the proposal to levy rates before completion of the works would be only to the benefit of the railway company. The contrast between the resources of the small company and the scale of their project was also noted. Three jetties were built; that furthest up-river, equipped with a double track to the end of the pier, was significantly larger than the others. The lines of quays along the shore did not materialise.

The Lostwithiel and Fowey Railway enjoyed good traffic in its earlier years. The records show that returns for 1872, 1873 and 1874 were 28,932 tons, 29,055 and 27,463 respectively. Returns for the following year of 8,979 tons, reflect the decisive impact of the CMR working in direct competition with the L&F Tonnage for 1877 showed a small recovery to 11,136, but by 1879 it had fallen back to only 7,921 tons. Depression within the china clay industry was also a further important factor here adversely affecting all rail movement of clay.

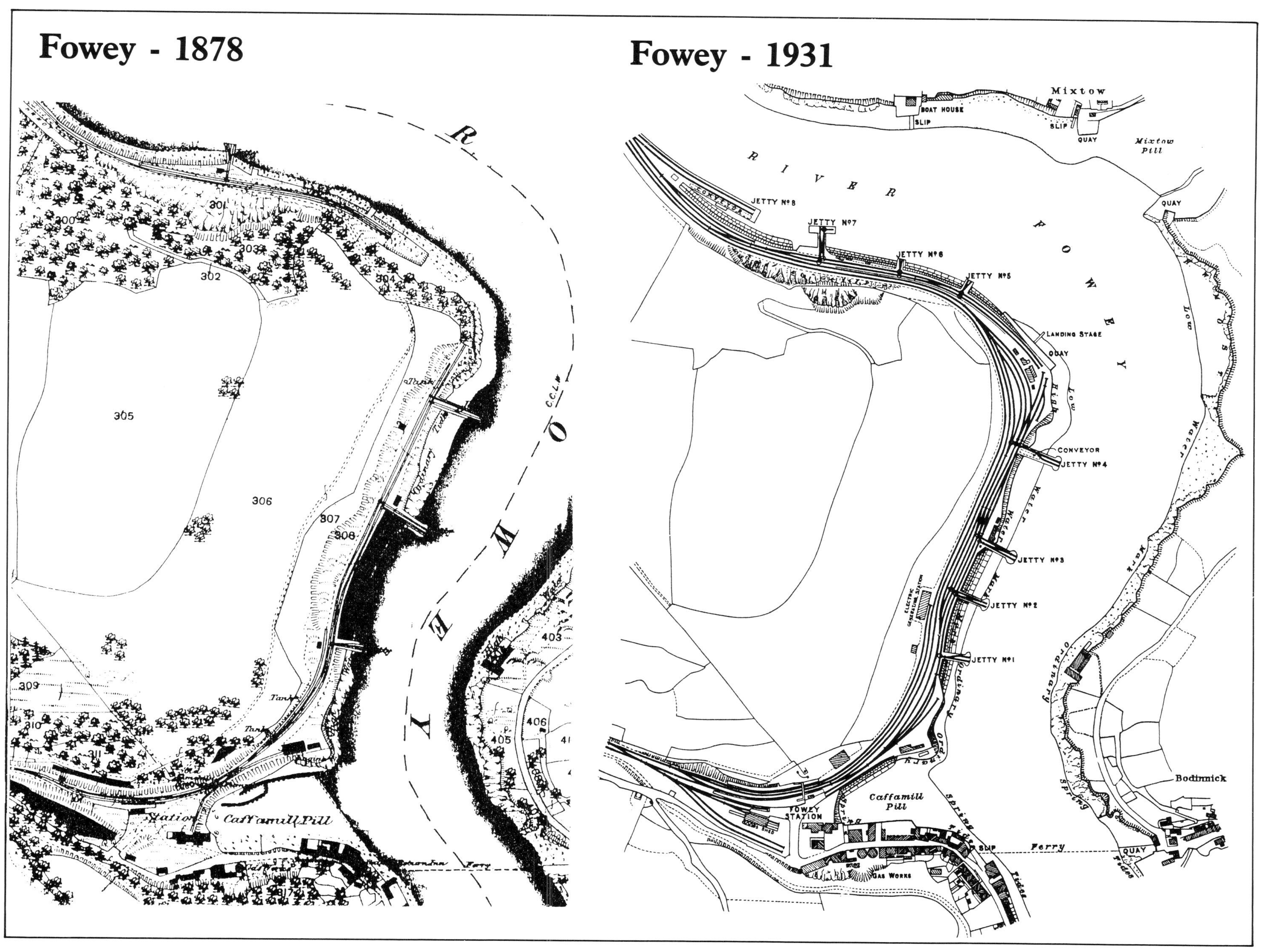

Fowey - 1878
Fowey - 1931
RIVER FOWEY
Mixtow
BOAT HOUSE
SLIP
QUAY
Mixtow Pill
JETTY Nº8
JETTY Nº7
JETTY Nº6
JETTY Nº5
LANDING STAGE
CONVEYOR
JETTY Nº4
JETTY Nº3
JETTY Nº2
JETTY Nº1
ELECTRIC GENERATING STATION
Low Water Mark
High Water Mark
Ordinary Spring Tides
Caffamill Pill
FOWEY STATION
GAS WORKS
Ferry
Bodinnick
R O W E Y
300
301
302
303
304
305
306
307
308
309
310
311
403
405
406
Tank
Station
Caffamill Pill

No. 1419 again, this time running alongside the magnificent River Fowey at low tide. The railway ran southward along the west bank of the river offering passengers an extremely attractive journey at all times of the year and at every stage of the tide. 22nd September 1959. *P.Q. Treloar*

The CMR was obviously a much larger concern than the L&F with detailed plans for harbour development at Fowey. Three large wooden jetties supported by timber piles were constructed 100 yards apart. The jetties were numbered 1 – 3 and were 90, 104 and 114 feet long respectively (see plan) reaching northward from Caffamill Pill towards Carne Point. At the seaward end of each jetty was a cage filled with stones to support the tipping apparatus as designed by Sir William Armstrong. Double track lines were also laid on each of the jetties, and at low water on a spring tide the depth was 23 feet for the ships alongside. The Pill or pool on the edge of Fowey harbour was also filled in part to make an embankment for railway access along the quays. Blast furnaces were planned close to the station but were never built.

Further developments reflect the growth of trade by the opening years of the present century. The Lostwithiel and Fowey Railway had earlier entered into a ruinoustrade battle with the CMR, undercutting the latter's rates for clay traffic. This ended in financial disaster for the Lostwithiel company to the extent that the line became unsafe for operation and was closed from 31st December 1879 to 16th September 1895. When reopened, after reconstruction to the standard gauge, it was extended to Fowey station, linking with the CMR. In the following year the Great Western Railway assumed full control of the Minerals Company, this taking effect from 1st July.

The new single line curve into Fowey (see map) linked the two sets of jetties. Those of the former L&F interests were extended, whilst siding accommodation was improved significantly. A quay was also built on the land that had originally separated the two railways and was also connected by rail. The 1908 map shows seven jetties in operation; numbers four and seven being the largest, and numbers five and six, the smallest. In 1909 No. 4 jetty was equipped with an elevator and conveyor belt powered by electricity; an obvious improvement on tipping and loading casks by crane.

Fowey handled an extensive export trade by the turn of the century with production levels in the Cornish clay pits reaching a peak in 1912 of 856,239 tons; 73,284 tons being china stone. Exports shipped from Fowey in 1886, for example, were recorded at 114,496 tons; ten years later the figure had more than doubled to 263,552 tons. The overall exports from all ports to foreign countries and colonies in 1912 stood at 661,300 tons; the impressive list of customers included Russia, Germany, Netherlands, Belgium, France, Italy, the United States and Canada, and India. Of these the United States and Germany were the largest markets, their imports being valued at £304,948 and £100,298 respectively. Fowey handled the bulk of this traffic. With the outbreak of war in August 1914, however, trade was dislocated and declined rapidly. By 1918 it was slightly in excess of 400,000 tons but valuable markets had been lost in Europe and with the emergence of the post-war society exports were checked by protective tariffs in many instances.

Par harbour seen from the air and looking northwards. Note the sailing ships awaiting their cargo and the high tide in this obviously tidal port. Fowey as a deep water anchorage had a great advantage over Par. A china clay dry can be seen immediately north of the harbour, whilst to the right is the low stone viaduct carrying the main line, east-west. Running beneath the viaduct and away to the right is the former Cornwall Minerals system with St Blazey depot and yard occupying an extensive area of land. Today the harbour looks very different, the result of considerable development in the 1960s. The railway presence has inevitably diminished here with lorry traffic handling traffic to the port. *English China Clays*

Par

Par harbour was served by both the Cornwall Minerals line and that of the Associated Companies, later the GWR. The harbour had been built by J.T. Treffry by 1840 enclosing an area of 35 acres. Considerable traffic came from copper ore raised from Fowey Consols mine nearby; coal, timber and lime were also important. Treffry's tramroad from Ponts Mill to Molinnis also encouraged traffic in china clay and granite. Par, however, did not possess the deep water of Fowey and was a tidal port. A vast rectangular reservoir or sluice pond was situated at the inward end of the quay. This helped keep the channel serving the quay as free as possible from mud. Rails were laid along the length of the main quay and a lead smelting works operated closeby until 1885. By the early twentieth century a flour mill replaced the smelter and a brick works was in production. Both were served by rail. On the smaller west quay opposite was a timber yard and a saw mill. Clay traffic from Par was comparable with other ports such as Charlestown, but was far below that of Fowey.

Traffic increased considerably after 1932, and from 1933 to 1940 was maintained at over 100,000 tons annually. In 1932 61,841 tons of clay passed through the port. The harbour was given new opportunities for trade in 1946 when it was leased by ECLP. The company bought the port in 1964 by which time it had been well developed to cater for the valuable European trade. By the end of the decade the port was able to handle up to one million tons of clay annually. Lloyd's List described Par as 'the busiest small port in the country'.

Fowey has also seen considerable progress and change since 1945. The main alterations here came in 1968 when the docks were taken over by the china clay company. Since that date much has been accomplished with the provision today of five jetties handling the export trade.

Number 8 Jetty:
served by rail direct.
Number 6 Jetty:
served by rail via a conveyor.
Number 5 Jetty:
handling bagged consignments served only by road.
Number 4 Jetty:
served by rail via a conveyor.
Number 3 Jetty:
a special berth for slurry traffic.

All the jetties are served by road. Returning to 1968, that year also saw the closure of the rail link between Par and Fowey. It was then converted to a roadway for the exclusive use of lorry traffic moving to and from the port, ending the monoply by rail services which then dated back almost a century.

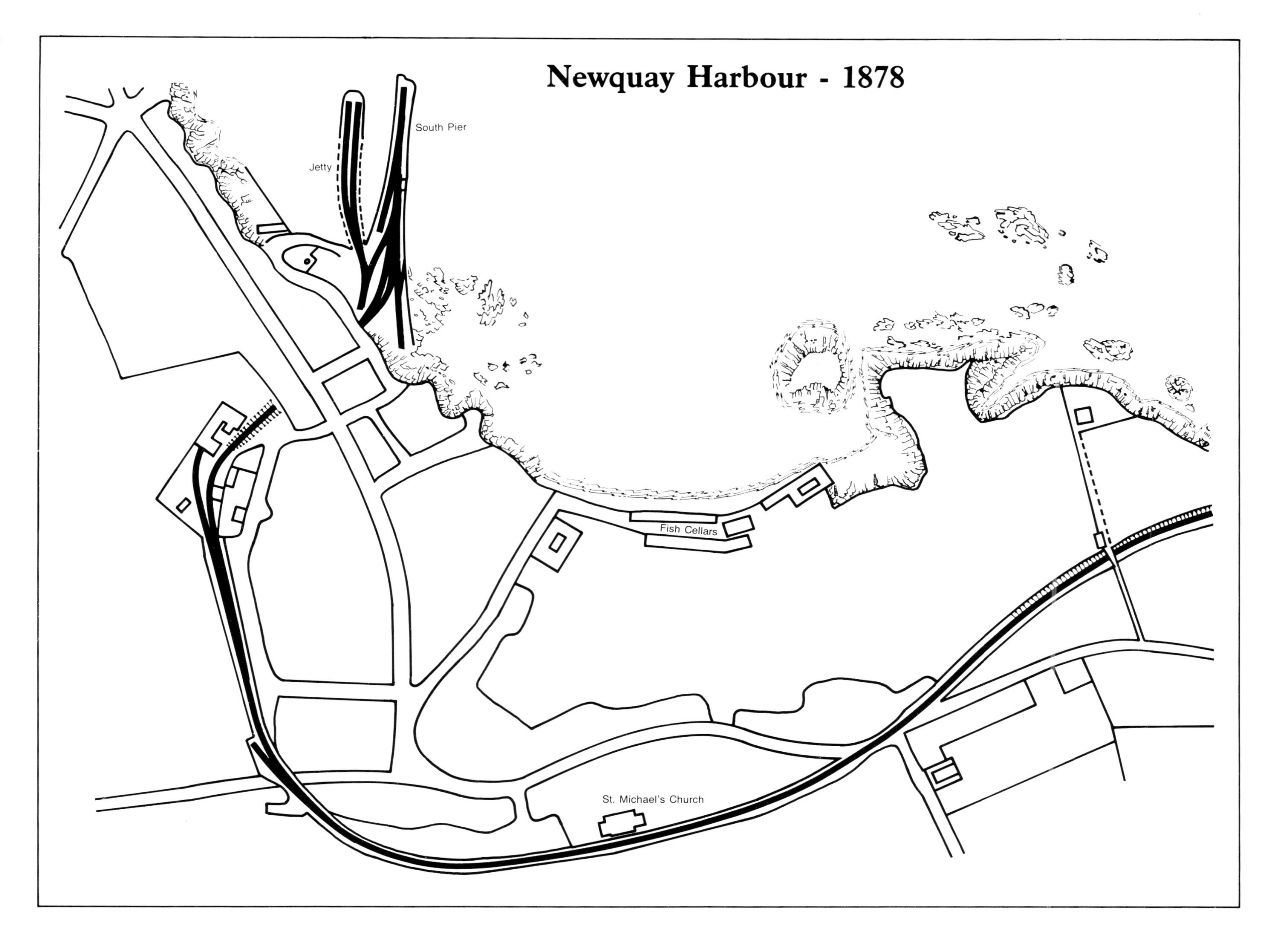

Newquay Harbour - 1878
South Pier
Jetty
Fish Cellars
St. Michael's Church

Newquay, on the north coast. This view from the early years of this century shows the harbour still drawing a living as a trading port. The railway reached the harbour by a tunnelled incline on a gradient of 1 in 4½. The central pier standing within the harbour and reached by the trestle bridge was built by the Cornwall Minerals Railway in 1872. Rails were earlier laid on the south pier under J.T. Treffry's tramroad system of 1849 linking the harbour with the clay district inland at Hendra and the lead mines at East Wheal Rose. Treffry had carried out the development of the harbour itself from 1838-1842. Note the presence of the large Atlantic Hotel and the paddle steamer, indicating the rise of a popular holiday resort.

Redruth Local Studies Library

Newquay

Newquay harbour was purchased by J.T. Treffry in 1838 and was extensively improved over the five year period to September 1842. This development made the north coast a somewhat less dangerous prospect than before particularly with the opening of Trevose Head lighthouse east of the port in December 1847.

The harbour was served by the tramroads from Hendra (St Dennis) and East Wheal Rose mine, opened in 1849, and was reached at Newquay itself via a tunnel on an incline of 1 in 4½ leading out onto the quay itself. In 1872 the Cornwall Minerals Company built a stone jetty within the harbour, 100 feet long and 20 feet wide. It was served by the railway with access provided by a wooden trestle structure 150 feet long. Two ships could use the new island jetty together thereby extending accommodation considerably. Rails were already laid along the south pier under the earlier development of 1849.

As a china clay port Newquay was not particularly important. It did, of course, serve the clay industry and various other trades, but it was always restricted because of its difficult location. As mentioned the north coast was always inhospitable to shipping despite many efforts at improvements. Extensions to the harbour would pose considerable problems by comparison with the south coast locations much preferred overall. The rail link from Newquay station yard to the harbour was finally closed in 1926, by which time the town was a leading holiday resort.

NEWQUAY.

To CAPITALISTS, BUILDERS and others.

MARINE RESIDENCES.

The Trustees of the TREFFRY ESTATE, are prepared to grant LEASES for 99 Years absolute, of several eligible building sites at Newquay, for the erection of Dwellinghouses of a Superior Class.

The Buildings to be approved by the Architect of the Estate.

From the bracing character and well known great salubrity of the air of Newquay, and the fact of the Town being now about to be connected with other parts of the County by Railway, eligible building sites are daily increasing in demand and value.

Chapter Nine

St. Blazey - Workshops & Yard

As an independent company, the CMR maintained its own locomotive depot, workshops and offices at Par. These were developed on wasteground to the north-east of Par village alongside the alignment of Treffry's canal linking Ponts Mill and the harbour.

Originally the site covered an area approximately 660 yards long and 100 yards wide. The main buildings included the fan-shaped locomotive shed. 202 feet in length and 75 feet wide, giving accommodation to eighteen locomotives on nine roads, each leading out to the turntable. An erecting and repair shop formed part of the overall complex, this being 122 feet by 80 feet; there was also a fitting shop 101 feet by 40 feet, and a smithy of 112 feet by 40 feet containing eight fires. A boiler house 40 feet by 25 feet and a water tower holding 2,500 gallons was also included. Away northward of the locomotive shed/workshop area was a wagon shop, 200 feet by 50 feet with an engine house accom-

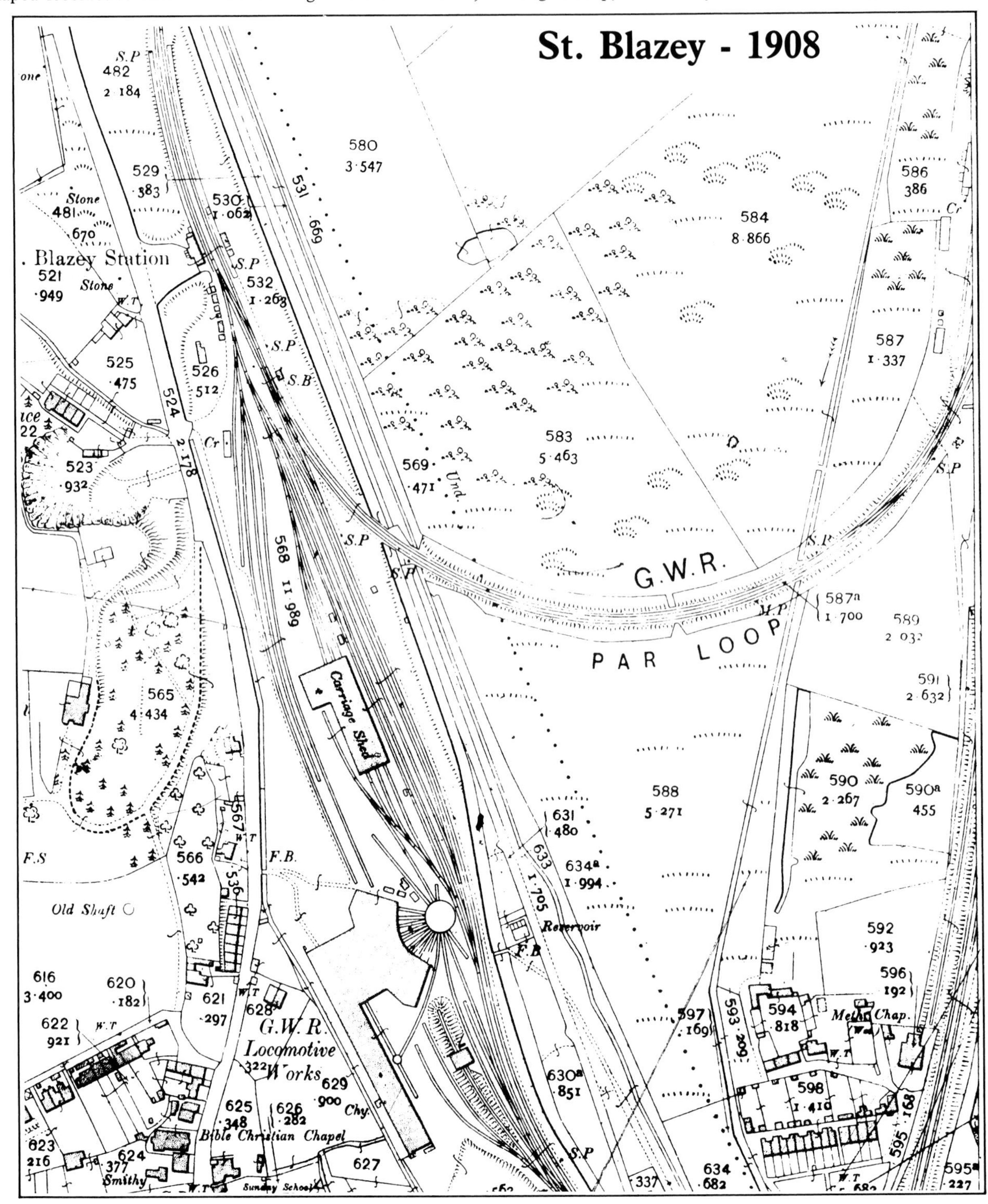

'4575' class 2-6-2T No. 5526 near Middleway Crossing, having passed through the busy yard at St. Blazey on 5th July 1955. The train is an evening working to Newquay.
R.C. Riley

'1600' class 0-6-0PT No. 1626 with a short freight mainly of clay wagons passes St. Blazey station and signal box. In the distance, at the south end of the yard, can be seen the buildings of the CMR wagon works and the locomotive shed. St. Blazey station closed to passengers in 1925.
R.C. Riley

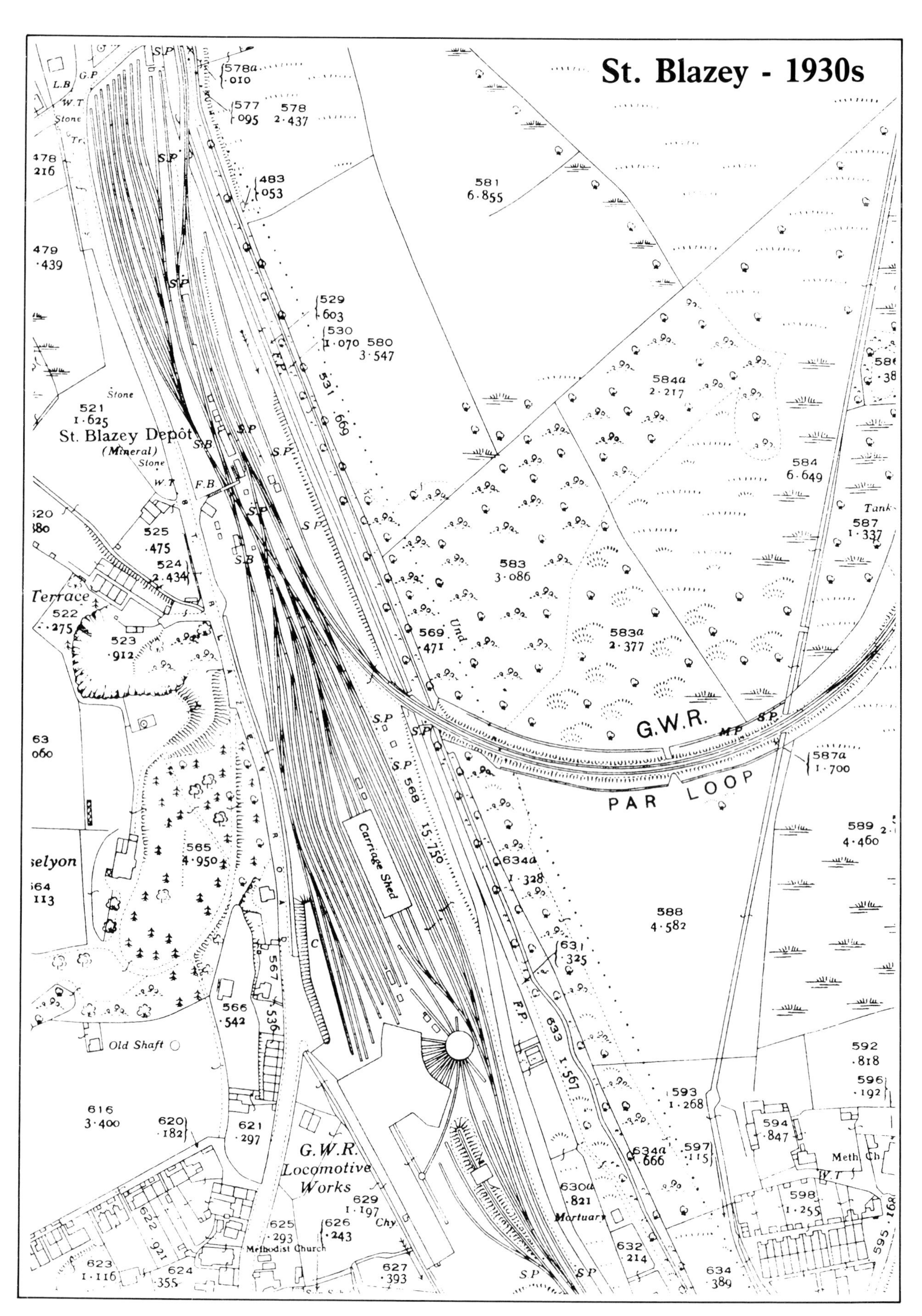
St. Blazey - 1930s
St. Blazey Depôt
(Mineral)
Terrace
Carriage Shed
G.W.R.
PAR LOOP
G.W.R. Locomotive Works
Methodist Church
Mortuary
Old Shaft
Meth. Ch.
Stone
Tank

modated alongside, measuring 50 feet by 30 feet. All construction was of brick, this being supplied from Plymouth. Further north along the yard, and opposite the access to the 1879 loop to Par station (GWR) was a goods shed. Beyond this again was Par station (CMR) renamed St Blazey in January 1879 to avoid confusion. Like all stations on the line there was a crossing loop, the main buildings being on the 'up' (east-side) platform.

By the early twentieth century there were detailed changes in siding accommodation. The 1908 plan shows the goods shed to have disappeared, it being replaced by a platform fitted with a crane. Three long sidings running southward almost to the locomotive shed were added on the land west of the wagon shop. Access to these was from the original alignment to the goods shed. The wagon shop itself was now served by extra lines; three through tracks being provided and a siding laid to the west of the building. At the locomotive shed, the turntable had been provided with extra access and bays. There were now two lines of access from the south, the Fowey direction, and one opposite leading towards the wagon shop. A coaling stage on its embankment was also added in the shed yard where, again, accommodation was increased. A signalbox was also provided at the west end of the Par loop between the railway and the river.

Plans for the mid thirties show further extensive development. The siding accommodation to the west of the wagon shop was both extended and increased. Eleven sets of rails now extended down to the north wall of the locomotive depot, but they were not all of the same length. North of St Blazey station (closed on 21st September 1925) and to the west of the line to Newquay, land was developed for further sidings. Nine lines were added, with access to the west of St Blazey station. Both this and the wagon shop were now surrounded by sidings, with a footbridge giving access to the station. The layout as developed by the years leading into World War Two showed, in traffic and capacity, the value of the clay trade to Cornwall.

Despite the somewhat reduced extent of the operation of St Blazey following rationalisation and the impact of road transport, the yard today retains considerable importance. The locomotive shed and wagon repair shop provides a continuous link with the opening to traffic well over a century ago, whilst investment in new rolling stock indicates a real commitment to the future.

Motive power for the minerals company was provided initially through an order for eighteen 0-6-0 side tank locomotives built by the 'Atlas' works of the Sharpe-Stewart Company of Manchester. They were designed by F. Trevithick. These locomotives were fitted with outside cylinders and 3ft 6in driving wheels, and weighed 32 tons 16 cwt. They were operated in pairs, back to back, but were not fitted with bunkers. Rebuilding took place from 1883 and at the 'grouping' seven were listed. Nine locomotives overall were inherited by the GWR when they took control of the company; the remainder being returned to the builders to be sold elsewhere. Those taken into Great Western stock were numbers 1392-1400. Class '850' 0-6-0 saddle tanks from the Great Western's Wolverhampton Works also worked the line at the turn of the century.

Par, or technically, St Blazey depot, always had a large allocation of tank engines for work on the clay branches. These were essential given the problems of restricted access, weight limitations and severe curvature. Churchward's famous '4500' class 2-6-2 tanks introduced in 1906 and the modified version with increased water supply, the '4575' class of 1924, were closely associated with the depot and its work until the final days of steam in 1962. The much larger and powerful Churchward '4200' class 2-8-0 tanks of 1910 worked the heavier services to and from Fowey. Collet's numerous '5700' class pannier tanks of 1929 after the design of the early '2021' class 0-6-0 were also allocated, as were limited numbers of Collett's larger '5100' class 2-6-2 tanks introduced in 1928. The lightweight Hawksworth '1600' class 0-6-0 pannier were likewise usefully employed on the branches. Collett's '1400' 0-4-2 class were given auto train duties on the Lostwithiel – Fowey services.

Churchward Moguls, the '4300' class 2-6-0, found duties at St Blazey whilst on summer Saturdays 'Castles', 'Counties', 'Halls' and later, the classes '22', '42' and '43' diesel hydraulics were all regularly employed on holiday services to and from Newquay. Over the steepest section, that from Par to Luxulyan, a 'Castle' assisted by a banker could take 320 tons maximum, with an increase to 450 tons coupled to a '4500' class with banking assistance also. Double-headed workings into Newquay were halted short of the terminus at Tolcarne Junction to detach the leading locomotive. This practice was also followed at Penzance with the leading locomotive on a double-headed train coming off at Marazion. This was necessary at Newquay and Penzance in order for the remaining locomotive to clear the points and run-round its train in the station itself.

Exchanging the token at St Blazey Bridge Crossing 22nd May 1959. A short, mixed, freight headed by '5700' class No. 9655 makes its way to St Blazey yard, with the fireman seen here ready to deal with the token. *M. Mensing*

Chapter Ten

Newquay Tourist Traffic

'We feel sure that the extension of the railway system to Newquay will attract thousands of visitors to our beautiful beaches and magnificent cliffs, and materially contribute to the prosperity of the neighbourhood.'

With this and other similar statements the people of Newquay officially welcomed the beginning of passenger services to the town on 20th July 1876. The first train started from Fowey on the Tuesday morning and was greeted with celebrations all along the line. As always, there were the local dignitaries, including Mr Richardson, the CMR General Manager, and Mr Constantine, the locomotive superintendant who drove the train. The St Blazey Band joined the train at Par to travel to Newquay, and at Victoria (Roche) the local school children were assembled on one platform and the general public on the other. A salute of fog signals was arranged and the vicar read an 'Address', welcoming the new service. At Newquay the train received 'a perfect ovation'; the entire community turning out in welcome, including the Foresters and Oddfellows, the coastguard and lifeboatmen.

The Cornwall Minerals Railway, in opening their services, also expressed optimism, predicting that 'under favourable circumstances, Newquay would become a second Torquay'. As a potential resort, Newquay had a great deal to recommend it. With the direct support of the Great Western Railway, who worked the CMR system from 1st October 1877, controlling it outright from 1st July 1896, tourism made good progress. The train service for 1876 is given here.

Prior to the opening of the connecting curve, brought into use of 1st January 1879, an omnibus service was provided for passengers between the Cornwall Railway's station and that of the CMR at Par. The timetable was also designed to give the best possible connections for 'up' and 'down' trains on the Cornwall line. The early departure from Newquay, for example, connected

Seaside holidays! Newquay's Towan Beach seen here on a busy summer's day either shortly before, or, soon after World War Two. On the right immediately above the sands is the promenade and theatre, opened in 1928, adding to the character and appeal of the beach generally. Just offshore is the small island complete with connecting bridge for the household. On the beach itself, off the far end of the promenade, is the almost natural swimming or paddling pool for children, whilst those people in the sea itself are enjoying Newquay's undoubted reputation for its excellent surf. For those less adventurous the grassed area above the beach offers a good opportunity to sit and enjoy the view seawards. Note the well-placed and more moderate hotel accommodation when compared with some of the much larger structures dating from the late Victorian and Edwardian eras.

Redruth Local Studies Library

with the Paddington service which arrived at Par at 8.04 and Paddington at 6pm.

Before the introduction of passenger services to Newquay, the GWR promoted a four horse bus service (1st May 1876) from Newquay to St Columb conveying passengers and mail. The coach then connected with a further service to Grampound Road station on the main line with a return working provided during the evening. The GWR arranged facilities for passengers to book at Newquay or St Columb for any station on its system.

The last quarter of the nineteenth century saw important steps in the transformation of Newquay from a small fishing and trading community into a recognised resort. A gas company was formed in 1878, and a water company four years later. A detailed sanitary programme also got underway during 1875 as part of the plan to create a modern, fashionable centre, the Local Board of Health receiving £3,000 from the Public Works Loan Commissioners to finance improvements. Further substantial developments with regard to water supply, drainage and sanitation also took effect at the turn of the century and in the years immediately prior to World War One. Much of Newquay's water supply was actually brought to the town in pipes laid along the course of the railway line itself; the source being located inland near Indian Queens.

By 1911 Newquay had a population of 4415; in contrast, it had been 1121 in 1871. Housing and hotels flourished. The best known hotels were the Atlantic, dating from 1890, The Great Western, 1878, The Hotel Victoria, 1899, the only hotel in England providing electric lifts from all floors to the beach below, and The Headland, 'the largest hotel in the West of England'. For its part, the GWR contributed £2,000 towards hotel development; the more exclusive accommodation mentioned here emphasising the modern amenities; electric lighting and lifts, telephones, 'the best sanitation' and attractions such as tennis, bowling greens, golf and the important proximity to the beaches. Significantly, the rateable value at Newquay increased from £5,050 in 1883 to £32,244 in 1914.

Newquay also had its obvious attractions for the rival London and South Western Railway. Their own publication *By Cornish Sea and Moors*, produced in 1915, gave full details of their services linking with North Cornwall. The North Cornwall Coach Company conveyed passengers between Wadebridge and Newquay and also offered access to the 'romantic scenery' of Boscastle and Tintagel rich in the Arthurian legend.

A useful addition to traffic locally came with the opening of the GWR Chacewater – Newquay branch via St Agnes and Perranporth on 2nd January 1905. This line did a great deal to open out tourism in West Cornwall giving good access to other resorts like Falmouth, Penzance and St Ives. It also played its part in what the 'West Briton' referred to as 'Newquay's second birth'. The town obviously felt a great sense of pride and achievement in the opening of the new line. In response to new opportunities the 'West Briton' recorded:

> 'Newquay people realise that the time for extra effort has arrived. The Council in turning its attention to the provision of a public park, and the scheme at Trenance Valley which has been under consideration for a couple of years is being hurried forward. The town is not encumbered by any debt and can afford to launch forth. The electric light is also to be installed by a private company.'

The terminus also benefitted from substantial improvements to coincide with the opening of the Chacewater route and the increase in traffic from other parts of Britain. A new island platform was provided enabling three trains to use the station when required; passenger facilities generally were also improved together with the extra provision for goods and locomotive sheds. A figure of £30,000 was given for these developments. Tolcarne Junction was also realigned (1904) with the addition of two sections of double track with loops; one section serving the route to Par, and the other, the new line to Perranporth and Chacewater.

Intermediate stations on the 20¾ mile section from Par and the main line were progressively renamed, with the exception of Bugle. Halloon became St Columb Road in December 1878, whilst Par, on the CMR, was renamed St Blazey in January 1879; Bridges became Luxulyan in May 1905 and Holywell became Victoria, and, finally, Roche in November 1904. Quintrell Downs was opened by the GWR in October 1911. All the stations had passing loops with the exception of the latter.

Finally, before leaving the formative years of the line, it needs to be said that prior to 1st January 1879 there were no effective links at all between the GWR and the CMR at Par. On that date a half mile curve was opened linking Par GWR with the minerals line yet until May 1892 and the abolition of the broad gauge, standard gauge 'branch' trains to Newquay stood alongside broad gauge main line services at Par. The removal of the broad gauge allowed through running to Newquay adding to the attraction for tourists, and encouraging the GWR to plan more ambitious services to and from the resort.

The inter-war years marked further progress enabling Newquay to establish itself as the county's premier tourist resort. Expenditure on publicity gave a good indication of growth. In 1926 for example, the town spent £130 on advertising; by 1935, with the direct assistance of the GWR this figure had risen to £1,000, this being considerably more than that of any other Cornish resort. Newquay's population was well over 8,000 by this time, being a community which, again, unlike other local resorts, was largely committed to a tourist economy. The Chamber of Commerce acknowledged the efforts of the GWR in stating that the company had 'taught them the use of advertising'. Newquay was also concerned with the 'Come to Cornwall Association', another initiative linked with the GWR dating from the 1920s. This encouraged a collective concern on the part of the resorts to promote tourism within the county.

The Great Western's *Ocean Coast* of May 1925 was also one of many company publications working to Newquay's advantage. Direct reference to invigorating Atlantic breezes, 'magnificent scenery, and charming resorts' well reflected Newquay's character. Of the *Ocean Coast* ideal the GWR stated:

> 'The Ocean Coast climate is most perfectly exemplified in Cornwall because that county is almost entirely surrounded by sea. Unless it comes straight down the one narrow neck of land, every wind must be a sea wind.'

The small Towan promenade was improved in 1928 with the provision of a theatre and shelters. This helped to open out access to the sea in the immediate town area. There were magnificent sea views from the headlands and cliffs beyond the town, but Newquay has always lacked a lengthy promenade like those at Falmouth and Penzance.

Publicity was all important. In 1938 members of the national and provincial press were invited to Newquay to promote the 'Easter Holiday Campaign', largely influenced by the GWR in order to extend the season more widely.

Holiday Haunts for 1938 shows representative third class monthly returns to Newquay as follows:-

Paddington	49s 1d
Birmingham	47s 9d
Sheffield	60s 11d
Manchester	61s 11d

Holiday Runabout tickets were also available on a weekly

Pounding their way up the 1 in 77 gradient, having just passed Quintrell Downs, 2-6-2T '5100' class No. 5198 pilots 'County' 4-6-0 No. 1002 *County of Berks* on the 11.15 am. Newquay-Wolverhampton. 9th July 1960. Eastbound trains, from Newquay, faced a long but less severe climb to the summit near Roche than those trains working to Newquay. Built as a mineral line, the Newquay branch presented many problems to the working of heavy passenger trains during summer. Harsh curvature and the steep gradients up to 1 in 40 on both sides of the summit made for interesting locomotive combinations as heavily loaded holiday trains of up to fifteen coaches struggled over the branch. *P. Gray*

basis, together with an extra service, the 'Specimen Newquay Tour'. This was as follows:

Saturday:
To Newquay, transfer to hotel, weekend at leisure.
Monday:
Whole day tour to Lands End/St Ives with luncheon at Lands End Hotel.
Tuesday:
At leisure in Newquay.
Wednesday:
Whole day tour to Looe and Polperro by coach.
Thursday & Friday:
At leisure in Newquay.
Saturday:
Return home train.

The introduction of the Holidays with Pay Act of 1938 proved an important development particularly for the post-war years when tourism flourished at Newquay. Success as a resort was by this time an imperative. Of all the Cornish tourist centres Newquay was now the most important; it was also unique in as far as its economy was almost entirely linked to the holiday industry. The population of the Newquay Urban District had grown by 8.2 per 1000 per annum between 1931 and 1939 as against a static situation at Penzance and increases at Truro and Falmouth of 3.6 and 1.9. The neighbouring area, particularly villages such as Cubert and Newlyn East, also grew rapidly between the two Wars, indicating the popularity of the area. Nearby Holywell Bay also grew as a resort. Census returns for the thirty year period 1931-61 further reflected Newquay's growth:- 1931 – 7,651; 1951 – 9,930; 1961 – 11,881.

The branch and the terminus itself were also improved with the development of tourism. The Goonbarrow Junction to Bugle section was provided with double track from July 1930, and Bugle station was rebuilt on a new alignment. The crossing loops at all the stations, except, of course, Quintrell Downs, were lengthened considerably during the 1930s whilst, earlier, in August 1921, the section from Tregoss Moor to St Dennis Junction was doubled. This latter section was to the east of St Dennis Junction itself and was almost two miles long.

Newquay station was further extended and the yard enlarged to cope with the increased summer traffic, work beginning in 1938. World War Two delayed things but by March 1946 the section from Tolcarne Junction into Newquay station was doubled, and a new signalbox was provided off the end of the new platforms, to the west of the line. The triangle at Tolcarne had been

'Manor' class 4-6-0 No. 7816 *Frilsham Manor* Pilots No. 6832 *Brockton Grange* up the Luxulyan Valley on the 10.05 am Par-Newquay. The reason for a double-header on a train of only three coaches was to provide an extra locomotive at Newquay for a return working on an eastbound holiday express. On the heaviest trains of thirteen, or even fourteen coaches, a double-headed train could expect assistance from the rear by a '4500' class tank. A 45mph speed restriction applied between Par and Newquay with many limits as low as 15 mph. *P. Gray*

reinstated in 1931 to enable tender locomotives to turn, the section involved, being the old east curve that originally gave direct access from the Fowey direction into the line to Shepherds and the mining district. One further major improvement to the branch must be recorded this being the rebuilding of Trenance viaduct, immediately outside Newquay. During 1938/1939 the single track structure here was replaced by a double track masonry viaduct built around the earlier stone piers.

The GWR planned to spend altogether some £80,000 at the terminus in carrying out its extension programme. Land was to be purchased on both sides of the line in the station area, and, on the west side of the line, over the whole distance to Tolcarne Junction. The platforms were extended, as at Penzance, to accommodate the heaviest holiday trains that the line could carry, and the original station yard and goods area was remodelled and extended to provide the necessary siding space for holiday trains. Should it be necessary, the yard could offer eleven lines for coaching stock, the seven most westerly of these being the main accommodation.

Tourist traffic increased considerably in the post-war period, the 1938 Holidays with Pay Act proving a major incentive. Newquay certainly had a great deal to offer its visitors in the shape of its magnificent beaches, coastal scenery, parks, gardens and recreational features – theatre, cinema, boating, golfing and tennis. Its popularity, however, gave rise to serious discussion on improvements to transport. In the late 1930s there were considerations of a regular air service and detailed concern about the development of the road system; there were also telling criticisms of rail services. Heavy summer trains frequently required not only double-heading but banking also. The improvements of the inter-war years eased traffic problems, but the severe limitations of a mineral line imposed working restrictions that could not be entirely overcome short of reconstruction. In fact, the local press carried details of a suggested scheme discussed by the GWR for a new line, as was the case with the Looe branch.

Rail services were not, however, seriously challenged until the late 1950s by which time holiday traffic on the branch had reached its peak.

The line continues to enjoy its distinction of being the only Cornish branch to carry through services in the summer months, but traffic over the branch in winter is sparse. All the intermediate stations along the line are now no more than unstaffed halts whilst Newquay itself reflects both times present and past. Of the platforms extended to meet heavy traffic requirements between the wars, one is now ruinous beyond the main station area, the other, the island platform, has lost its canopy. The sidings have been shortened to make way for the inevitable car park, whilst outside, on the main road, the railway presence has all but disappeared; the station entrance now forming part of an anonymous modern street development.

Further evidence of decline came with the end of the summer timetable 1987. Officially all locomotive hauled services ended on Saturday 3rd October but the following day saw a special working from Paddington to mark the event. The motive power in this case were Nos. 50034 *Furious* and 50035 *Ark Royal*. One week later, on Saturday 10th October, the signalbox and booking office/travel centre closed. Summer through workings for 1988 are handled by I.C.125 sets, with a ground frame replacing the signalbox. Newquay today is a flourishing modern holiday centre and although the railway is clearly no longer the vital force it once was, its role in the overall development of the resort has been decisive.

TIMETABLE MAY 1859

SHOWING ALSO CONNECTING SERVICES WITH PENZANCE

EASTWARD		Weekdays
		dep. TRURO 5.45 am for PLYMOUTH arr. 8.35 am PADDINGTON arr 9.15 pm
PZ dep.	6.15 am	arr. TRURO 8.05 am
		dep. TRURO 8.20 am for PLYMOUTH arr. 10.30 am PADDINGTON arr. 6.00 pm
PZ dep.	8.55 am	arr. TRURO 10.45 am
		dep. TRURO 11.00 am for PLYMOUTH arr. 1.50 pm BRISTOL arr. 8.50 pm
PZ dep.	1.45 pm	arr. TRURO 3.35 pm
		dep. TRURO 3.50 pm for PLYMOUTH arr. 6.40 pm PADDINGTON arr. 4.45 am MAIL
PZ dep.	4.35 pm	Passengers and Goods arr. TRURO 6.35pm
		dep. TRURO 6.55 pm for PLYMOUTH arr. 9.45 pm
PZ dep.	7.44 pm	arr. TRURO 9.34 pm (Newham terminus, West Cornwall Railway.)
		Sundays
		dep. TRURO 6.50 am for PADDINGTON arr. 10.20 pm
PZ dep.	9.09 am	arr. TRURO 10.59 am
		dep. TRURO 3.50 pm for PADDINGTON arr. 12.25 am MAIL
PZ dep.	7.05 pm	arr. TRURO 8.55 pm

WESTWARD		Weekdays
PZ arr.	8.40 am	dep. TRURO 6.50 am (Newham terminus)
PZ arr.	11.00 am	arr. TRURO 8.55 am
		dep TRURO 9.10 am from PLYMOUTH 6.05 am PADDINGTON dep. 8.10 pm MAIL
PZ arr.	3.37 pm	arr. TRURO 1.05 pm
		dep. TRURO 1.37 pm from PLYMOUTH 10.10 am EXETER dep. 6.55 am
PZ arr.	7.05 pm	arr. TRURO 5.00 pm
		dep. TRURO 5.15 pm from PLYMOUTH 2.05 pm BRISTOL dep. 7.50 am
PZ arr.	9.35 pm	arr. TRURO 7.30 pm
		dep. TRURO 7.45 pm from PLYMOUTH 5.20 pm PADDINGTON dep. 9.30 am
		arr. TRURO 10.20 pm from PLYMOUTH 7.25 pm PADDINGTON dep. 6.00 am
		Sundays
PZ arr.	11.00 am	arr. TRURO 8.55 am
		dep. TRURO 9.10 am from BRISTOL dep. 12.40 am MAIL
PZ arr.	8.56 pm	arr. TRURO 5.00 pm
		dep. TRURO 7.06 pm from BRISTOL dep. 7.50 am

PAR – NEWQUAY BRANCH – 1905

		WEEK DAYS ONLY.							
		a.m.		a.m.	p.m.	p.m.	p.m.	p.m.	
PAR	dep.	6 5	Mixed.	9 10	12 52	5 20	7 50	*9 55*	Saturdays Only.
St. Blazey	,,	6 9		9 15	1 2	5 24	7 56	*10 0*	
Luxulyan	,,	X		9 27	1 13	5 35	8 9	*10 11*	
Bugle	,,	...		9 36	1 19	5 40	8 15	*10 16*	
Roche	,,	6 34		9 42	1 28	5 50	8 22	*10 24*	
St. Columb Road... ...	,,	7 0		9 56	1 42	6 5	8 35	*10 38*	
NEWQUAY	arr.	7 18		10 10	1 55	6 20	8 47	*10 50*	

		WEEK DAYS ONLY.					
		a.m.	a.m.	p.m.	p.m.	p.m.	
NEWQUAY	dep.	8 50	11 15	12 55	5 25	*8 20*	Saturdays Only.
St. Columb Road ...	,,	9 2	11 30	1 11	5 39	*8 35*	
Roche	,,	9 18	11 44	1 26	5 53	*8 50*	
Bugle	,,	9 25	11 51	1 33	6 0	*8 58*	
Luxulyan	,,	9 30	11 57	1 39	6 6	*9 4*	
St. Blazey	,,	9 44	12 13	1 52	6 20	*9 18*	
PAR	arr.	9 47	12 15	1 54	6 23	*9 20*	

X—Calls at Luxulyan to set down Passengers from London on notice being given by the Passenger to the Guard at Par.

CHACEWATER, PERRANPORTH AND NEWQUAY.

RAIL MOTOR CAR—ONE CLASS ONLY.

		WEEK DAYS ONLY.								
		a.m.	a.m.	p.m.	p.m.	p.m.	p.m.		p.m.	
CHACEWATER ...	dep.	7 55	10 7	12 30	2 35	4 26	6 25	...	*8 48*	Saturdays Only.
Mount Hawke ...	,,	8 0	10 12	12 35	2 40	4 31	6 30	...	...	
St. Agnes	,,	8 5	10 17	12 40	2 45	4 36	6 35	...	*8 53*	
*Goonbell	,,	8 8	R	R	R	4 39	6 38	...	...	
*Mithian	,,	8 13	R	R	R	4 44	6 43	...	...	
PERRANPORTH	arr.	8 18	10 30	12 53	2 58	4 49	6 48	...	*9 9*	
	dep.	8 19	10 31	12 54	2 59	4 51	6 49	...	*9 10*	
*Goonhavern ...	,,	8 26	10 38	1 1	3 6	4 58	6 56	...	...	
Shepherds	,,	8 32	10 44	1 7	3 12	5 4	7 2	...	*9 22*	
*Mitchell & Newlyn	,,	8 36	10 48	1 11	3 16	5 8	7 6	...	...	
*Trewerry & Trerice	,,	8 41	10 53	1 16	3 21	5 13	7 11	...	...	
NEWQUAY ...	arr.	8 52	11 0	1 23	3 28	5 20	7 18	...	*9 38*	

		WEEK DAYS ONLY.								
		a.m.	a.m.	a.m.	p.m.	p.m.	p.m.		p.m.	
NEWQUAY ...	dep.	7 50	8 55	11 5	1 30	4 25	6 45	...	*7 40*	Saturdays Only.
*Trewerry & Trerice	,,	7 57	9 2	11 12	1 37	4 32	6 52	...	...	
*Mitchell & Newlyn	,,	8 2	9 7	11 17	1 42	4 37	6 57	...	...	
Shepherds	,,	8 6	9 11	11 21	1 46	4 41	7 3	...	*7 56*	
*Goonhavern ...	,,	8 11	9 16	11 26	1 51	4 46	7 8	...	...	
PERRANPORTH	arr.	8 15	9 20	11 30	1 55	4 50	7 12	...	*8 5*	
	dep.	8 26	9 21	11 31	1 56	4 53	7 13	...	*8 6*	
*Mithian	,,	8 35	R	R	R	5 3	7 22	...	...	
*Goonbell	,,	8 40	R	R	R	5 9	7 27	...	...	
St. Agnes	,,	8 43	9 38	11 48	2 13	5 13	7 30	...	*8 23*	
*Mount Hawke ...	,,	8 48	9 43	11 53	2 18	5 19	7 35	...	...	
CHACEWATER ...	arr.	8 53	9 48	11 58	2 23	5 25	7 40	...	*8 33*	

* These places are Halts. R These cars will call if required at Goonbell and Mithian to pick up and set down passengers.

FALMOUTH BRANCH – 1905

		WEEK DAYS.															SUNDAYS.				
		a.m.	a.m.	a.m.	p.m.	p.m.	p.m.	p.m.	p.m.	p.m.	p.m.						a.m.	a.m.	p.m.		
TRURO ...	dep.	6 35	9 50	11 55	1 35	2 25	3 55	5 30	6 12	8 30	10 30	...	...	...	...	...	6 35	9 33	6 8	...	...
Perranwell ...	,,	6 45	10 3	12 5	1 47	2 37	4 5	5 40	6 23	8 40	10 40	...	...	...	...	...	6 45	9 44	6 20	...	...
Penryn ...	,,	6 55	10 13	12 15	1 57	2 49	4 15	5 50	6 34	8 50	10 50	...	...	...	...	...	6 55	9 54	6 30	...	...
FALMOUTH ...	arr.	7 3	10 23	12 25	2 5	2 57	4 25	6 0	6 40	9 0	11 0	...	...	...	...	...	7 3	10 3	6 39	...	...
		a.m.	a.m.	a.m.	a.m.	p.m.	p.m.	p.m.	p.m.	p.m.	p.m.						a.m.	p.m.	p.m.		
FALMOUTH ...	dep.	7 10	8 35	9 10	11 5	12 45	2 40	3 20	5 20	6 55	9 20	...	...	...	...	...	8 45	3 10	5 20	...	...
Penryn ...	,,	7 19	8 45	9 19	11 14	12 55	2 48	3 28	5 30	7 3	9 30	...	...	...	...	...	8 55	3 20	5 30	...	...
Perranwell ...	,,	7 28	8 55	9 29	11 22	1 5	2 58	3 38	5 40	7 13	9 40	...	...	...	...	...	9 5	3 30	5 40	...	...
TRURO ...	arr.	7 39	9 5	9 39	11 33	1 15	3 8	3 48	5 50	7 24	9 50	...	...	...	...	...	9 15	3 39	5 50	...	...

PAR – NEWQUAY, PAR – FOWEY AND LOSTWITHIEL – FOWEY SERVICES IN 1909

	A.M.	A.M.	P.M.	P.M.	P.M.
Par	6.05	9.15	12.53	5.25	8.07
St. Blazey	6.09	9.20	1.00	5.29	8.10
Luxulyan	P	9.32	1.13	5.39	8.22
Bugle	–	9.41	1.19	5.44	8.30
Roche	6.34	9.47	1.28	5.51	8.36
St. Columb	7.00	10.00	1.42	6.05	8.49
Newquay	7.18	10.15	1.55	6.20	9.05

	A.M.	A.M.	P.M.	P.M.
Newquay	8.55	11.15	12.55	5.25
St. Columb	9.07	11.28	1.11	5.39
Roche	9.22	11.44	1.26	5.53
Bugle	9.29	11.51	1.33	6.00
Luxulyan	9.36	11.57	1.39	6.06
St. Blazey	9.48	12.11	1.52	6.20
Par	9.50	12.14	1.54	6.22

P Calls to set down London passengers on notice given to the guard at Par.

	A.M.	A.M.	P.M.	P.M.	P.M.
Par	9.15	10.05	12.53	5.25	6.55
St. Blazey	9.20	10.10	1.03	5.32	7.01
Fowey	9.32	10.23	1.15	5.44	7.13
Fowey	8.00	11.55	4.43	6.05	8.18
St. Blazey	8.15	12.11	4.58	6.20	8.35
Par	8.17	12.14	5.00	6.22	8.37

	A.M.	A.M.	P.M.	P.M.	P.M.
Lostwithiel	10.05	10.57	3.00	4.20	7.50
Golant	10.15	11.07	3.10	4.30	8.00
Fowey	10.20	11.12	3.15	4.35	8.05
Fowey	9.45	10.27	1.55	3.50	6.05
Golant	9.52	10.34	2.02	3.57	6.12
Lostwithiel	10.00	10.42	2.10	4.05	6.20

PAR – NEWQUAY SUMMER 1932 LOSTWITHIEL – FOWEY

	A.M.					P.M.		SX	SO	SO					SO
Par	5.55	6.30	7.35	9.26	10.25	12.05	2.22	4.10	–	4.25	5.08	6.10	7.40	8.05	10.55
Luxulyan	–	6.45		9.44	–	12.25	2.39	4.25	–	4.40	–	F	7.54	F	F
Bugle	–	6.51	7.55	9.49	10.47	12.32	2.44	4.31	–	4.46	5.28	F	8.00	F	F
Roche	–	6.58	8.00	9.55	–	12.39	2.50	4.37	–	4.52	5.35	F	8.07	F	F
St. Columb Road	6.25	7.15	8.15	10.09	11.08	12.55	3.04	4.52	–	5.06	5.50	6.45	8.21	8.41	11.28
Quintrell Down Platform	–	–	8.25	10.18	–	1.04	3.13	–	–	–	–	6.56	–	–	–
Newquay	6.40	7.27	8.32	10.25	11.25	1.10	3.20	5.05	5.05	5.20	6.03	7.03	8.35	8.55	11.40

SX – Sats excepted SO – Sats only F – Calls to set down passengers from Ply and beyond on notice to the guard given at Par

	A.M.				P.M.		SO	SX	SO				SO
Lostwithiel	7.15	8.55	10.20	11.35	12.38	2.40	4.20	4.55	5.15	6.30	7.45	9.25	11.00
Golant	7.24	9.04	10.29	11.44	12.47	2.49	4.29	5.04	5.24	6.39	7.54	9.34	11.09
Fowey	7.30	9.10	10.35	11.50	12.53	2.55	4.35	5.10	5.30	6.45	8.00	9.40	11.15

SUMMER SATURDAYS 1959

NEWQUAY DEPARTURES

Saturdays

7.50 am	Manchester London Road arr. 7.34 pm
8.05 am	Sheffield/Newcastle arr. Sheffield 6.31 pm; Newcastle 9.52 pm
10.00 am	Paddington arr. 4.55 pm
11.00 am	York arr. 11.14 pm
11.15 am	Birmingham/Wolverhampton arr. Birmingham 7.16 pm; Wolverhampton 7.58 pm
12.30 pm	Paddington arr. 7.25 pm
12.40 pm	Cardiff arr. 8.00 pm
1.45 pm	Paddington arr. 8.55 pm – 11 July – 29 August
6.00 pm	Plymouth arr. 8.15 pm

NEWQUAY ARRIVALS

Saturdays

5.50 am	Newcastle dep. 3.40 pm. Friday only.
6.15 am	Paddington dep. 10.50 pm. Friday only.
7.50 am	Wolverhampton dep. 9.50 pm. Fridays only to 4 Sept.
9.25 am	Manchester London Road dep. 9.15 pm. Friday only. 26 June – 21 August.
4.05 pm	Paddington dep. 8.25 am. (For Perranporth via Truro arr. 4.20)
4.30 pm	Paddington dep. 9.30 am
7.50 pm	Cardiff dep. 12.20 pm

Acknowledgements

Many people have helped in the preparation of this book and I would like the opportunity to thank them.

Firstly, I must mention my publisher, Roger Hardingham, for giving me the opportunity to get the material into print. Terry Knight and Joanne Hillman of the Local Studies Library at Redruth also deserve special mention for all their assistance, interest and encouragement; likewise the staff of the Royal Institution of Cornwall. I would also like to express my gratitude to Ivor Bowditch of 'English China Clays' for his and the Company's efforts on my behalf; the photographic material has proved to be invaluable, in illustrating the survey of the clay industry. Michael Messenger, a fellow railway historian must also be mentioned for making aspects of his own research on the clay lines available to me. Grateful thanks to John Joseph Design for the excellent diagrams.

Peter Gray, Michael Mensing and Peter Treloar have, once again, provided excellent photographs covering all aspects of the railway system in the latter days of steam working; the Local Studies Library and the Royal Institution have also provided valuable material covering the earlier years. Messrs. Roger Winnen and Graham Corin must also be thanked for allowing me the use of timetables, ancient and modern.

I must also thank Margaret Barron for her work in typing the manuscript and for handling numerous last-minute additions/alterations as extra material came available.

Finally, thanks to my wife, Jo, for her part in encouraging the project and for accompanying me on numerous visits to lineside locations, not of her choosing.